Advance Praise for Blending In

"Barbara Gowan honest life story delights, entertains and at times reminds us of our-selves. As the reader we learn of the confusion and "yearning to belong" that many adoptees experience. This book shares so beautifully how the reality of a person's accomplishments, personal character and achievements are only a partial make up of the multifaceted life of most adoptees. I encourage those whom are not adopted to read this book to closer comprehend the complexities of being adopted. This is exactly the reason this is a MUST read book for everyone that wishes to learn about human relationships. This book deepens the readers understanding that adoption is NOT a one-time occurrence in someone's life. I highly recommend this book to ALL adoptive parents, adoptees, birthparents and birthfamilies as well as those in the adop-tion support community. Most importantly I recommend this book to pre-adoptive parents. This book will help you to see into your child's heart before you ever meet him or her. This book will better you as a parent as well as your child."

—Sabra Cossentine,
Pioneer in Adoption Support Community via the Internet

"In a candid, honest, and emotionally connective life story, Barbara Gowan shares the story of a woman's quest for love, the loss of love, and finally finding real love in unexpected places. This is more than one woman's story of abuse and victory; it is the common struggle of life with the usual cast of characters: family, addictions, and unforeseen challenges. Through her journey of hurt, hope, and healing, Gowan painfully and prayerfully opens our eyes to how God works all things together for our good."

—Rev. Dr. Howard-John Wesley,
Senior Pastor of St. John's Congregational Church

"This memoir is an important contribution to understanding the profound and complex affects of adoption. Ms. Gowan's honest exploration of her life, racial-eth-nic heritage, and her pursuit of creating and connecting the many roots and branches of her family tree will hopefully provide insights to help adoptive parents, birthparents, and most importantly, adoptees."

—Gina M. Samuels,
PhD, School of Social Service Administration, University of Chicago

Blending In

✦

Crisscrossing the Lines of Race, Religion, Family, and Adoption

Barbara Ann Gowan

Lisa,

I hope you will be able to relate to my story & it will be a blessing to you. If you need someone to talk to you can reach me via my website www.blendingin.biz

With Love,
Barbara

iUniverse, Inc.
New York Lincoln Shanghai

Blending In
Crisscrossing the Lines of Race, Religion, Family, and Adoption

iUniverse books may be ordered through booksellers or by contacting:

iUniverse
2021 Pine Lake Road, Suite 100
Lincoln, NE 68512
www.iuniverse.com
1-800-Authors (1-800-288-4677)

Because of the dynamic nature of the Internet, any Web addresses or links contained in this book may have changed since publication and may no longer be valid.

The views expressed in this work are solely those of the author and do not necessarily reflect the views of the publisher, and the publisher hereby disclaims any responsibility for them.

ISBN: 978-0-595-44385-7 (pbk)
ISBN: 978-0-595-69834-9 (cloth)
ISBN: 978-0-595-88714-9 (ebk)

Printed in the United States of America

Contents

Acknowledgements ix

Introduction xiii

Part I   *Finding a Home*

CHAPTER 1   Who Am I? 3

Part II   *Finding Myself*

CHAPTER 2   Where Do I Fit in? 21

CHAPTER 3   Loving the Skin You're in 32

CHAPTER 4   Joy and Pain 45

CHAPTER 5   Codependency, Divorce, and Dating. 57

CHAPTER 6   New Beginnings 71

CHAPTER 7   Orphaned Again 83

Part III   *Finding My Faith*

CHAPTER 8   Accepting the Truth 95

Part IV   *Finding My Roots*

CHAPTER 9   Seeking My Roots 111

CHAPTER 10   The Black Side 124

CHAPTER 11   Learning and Growing. 149

Part V   Fulfilling My Purpose

CHAPTER 12   Enlarging My Territory 161

Epilogue 179

APPENDIX   Resources for Adoptive Families. 185

Acknowledgements

∘ ∘

I am your Creator. You were in my care even before you were born.

—*Isaiah 44: 2 CEV*

I thank God that He created me and has kept me in His care even before I knew Him.

I was listening to a sermon by Joel Osteen that talked about Divine connections. He spoke about how our destiny is connected to other people. Anyone can be a divine connection in your life and you can also be a divine connection and make a difference in someone else's life. What appears to be a chance meeting with one person can lead you to a major decision or a connection with another person. In thinking back over my life, I see so many instances when I was at the right place at the right time meeting the right person who would make a major impact on my life.

I thank God for sending Mr. and Mrs. Bland to care for me until my loving parents, Thelma and Harold Miller, adopted me.

I am also thankful for all of my extended family, including the many "aunties" who cared for me: Auntie June, Auntie Goodie, Aunt Tine, Aunt Alma, Aunt Dot, Aunt Audrey, also my special Godmother Claire.

I was blessed to find my birth father, who welcomed me into the Leflore family with open arms. I can't put into words how much the love and support I received from them has meant to me. I also need to thank my birth mother for the loving sacrifice of giving birth to me.

I was blessed with the miracle of four precious gifts from God, my children India, Brittany, JJ, and John. You are the most important gifts in my life.

I was not only adopted into the Miller family but also the Webb and Marshall families through my loving friends. I am eternally grateful to have such supportive, giving, encouraging, and nurturing friends in Veronica and Dawn. Their families have strengthened my spirit beyond expression.

I have also learned about God's love through my friends Michele, Dana, and Alicia. I am truly blessed in my friendships. I thank God for all of the friends I mention in this book as well as those who were equally important, including Cheryl Bass (both of them), my prayer partner Lenny, Vicki, Crystal, Janet, Evon, Brenda, and my many friends and coworkers in SC and MA.

I am thankful to all my teachers and those who have taught me about my Lord, especially Pastor Wesley and my loving congregation. I could not have made it through my valleys if not for their love, prayer, and support—especially from Emily, Mrs. Wise, Kim, Traci, Angela, Greg, Maxine, Sylvia, and Anna Hatchett.

I do believe "it is better to have loved and lost than never to have loved at all." I thank the special men in my life, and their families, who nurtured, loved, and helped me grow into the woman I have become. The highs and the lows taught me valuable lessons for which I am grateful.

This journey began when a friend said, "Maybe you should write a book." That comment led me to a conversation with author Sherrie Eldridge, who guided me and gave me a divine connection with Michelle Hughes. She, in turn, led me to other adoptees with stories to share and to other authors who would encourage and inspire me on this unfamiliar road. I couldn't have done this without all of their help.

I also couldn't have done it without the help and constant encouragement of my editor, Dale E. Parker. The Prayer of Jabez and her divine connection with the Marshall family brought us together. Her tireless effort is much appreciated. I would also like to thank Liza Dolensky for all of her input and effort as well.

I will finish as I began, giving thanks to God and to my Lord and Savior, Jesus Christ, for saving me and for blessing me with Life and bringing me Love through my friends and family. For without love, life is not worth living.

Give thanks to the Lord, for he is good; his love endures forever.

—Psalm 118

Introduction

It is my hope that this book inspires, encourages, or at least validates, the feelings of those struggling with the issues of family, race, or religion, especially those in the adoption community.

The reasons I wrote this book were numerous and ever changing. When I concluded my search for my birth family, I learned a lot about myself—and how I became the person that I am today. I shared my story with my friends, my family, and my church congregation. Their response was overwhelming. I didn't think my discoveries or my story would affect anyone outside the adoption community. I was wrong.

I came to realize that many people inside and outside of the adoption community struggle with the same issues of belonging as it relates to family, race, and religion as I did. Race and family are no longer concrete notions. Blended families, blended races, households with blended religions all are now commonplace.

I was encouraged to share my story with others as a testimony. During National Adoption Awareness Month in November 2004, I met with a local reporter and was featured in an article that ran front page in the Sunday Republican. The response to that article was even more overwhelming. I received many phone calls of encouragement as well as from those wanting my assistance with their own journey.

This book was to be a happy little reunion story. As time went on and I began writing my story, I had to confront the skeletons in my closet, many hidden family secrets, and come to terms with the fact that my life thus far was nothing like the Cinderella story. I came face to face with lifelong issues regarding belonging, trust, and identity.

The contents of the book have changed over time as I have allowed the Holy Spirit to guide my writing. This journey has been one of healing for me as I recall many happy and many more-painful events. Each had a lesson. Some I learned right away and some I learned over time. In hindsight, I have learned to be grateful for every experience—the good and the bad—because they all served a purpose. I am the person I am today because of these life experiences. I have learned to be content in whatever situation I am in.

Baring my soul was a very difficult task, but I feel I was called to share my story in the hope that it will minister to others.

It was equally hard to share parts of my life that included those close to me, but without their stories, my story would be incomplete. Several names have been changed, to protect and respect their privacy. Many of my milestones and life-changing events occurred while crisscrossing the lives of others. I hope their stories, as well as mine, will help you to reflect on your own life. Many people have touched me, but only those whose lives intersected mine in the areas of race, religion, and family are included, although the others are not forgotten.

I pray that as you take a walk in my shoes, you will learn something not only about my life, but reflect on yours as well—and be blessed as I have been blessed!

PART I
Finding a Home

1

Who Am I?

o o o o o o o o o o o o o o o o o o o o o o o o o o o o o o o o o o o
We don't see things as they are; we see them as we are.

—*Anais Nin*

A member of the adoption community once wrote, "Reunion is like a journey to a foreign country where one doesn't know the customs or the language." These thoughts flooded into my head as I relaxed on the beach in Negril, Jamaica. I was taking in the tranquility of the ocean waves and trying to ignore the pungent smell of marijuana in the distance. It was 6:30 AM in April of 2005.

I was reminiscing about the last six days of my spring vacation. My thoughts wandered from our voyage to the YS waterfalls and the fun we had jumping off a rope swing into the cool, clear water, to the Black River boat trip where we learned about the natural habitat of Jamaica and saw crocodiles swimming all around us, to the charming taxi driver who was our tour guide for much of our trip, to a sweet young lady bartender who told us just how hard it was to get a visa to travel to the United States. The people we came in contact with during our trip shared stories about their culture, their religion, and their lives.

An attractive black woman approached me while I was relaxing in my beach chair reading, one of the friendly, nameless vacationers I had waved or smiled at during my week in Jamaica.

"Do you have a camera with you?" she asked.

"No, but I usually carry it with me all of the time," I responded.

"I was watching you reading by the ocean and the serenity of that scene made me wish I could capture it on film for you."

I was pleasantly surprised by her comment and told her that she was very thoughtful to think of doing that for a stranger. We then struck up a lengthy conversation about our vacations and our life experiences. We shared many similar stories of our heritages including the roots of her family tree that, as with many African-American families, included a distant white relative.

I went on to tell her about an eerily similar conversation I had just the day before with a Jamaican woman who worked at a souvenir shop. This previous discussion started out about clothes and led to religious influences and biracial and multiracial identities in our respective countries. These related conversations about faith, race, and their effects on our families, made me wish I had more time to talk with both of these friendly, open, women. It also made me wonder if there is something about me that caused these topics to surface—or do other people simply think about them as much as I do?

I told both women that I had left my husband and four children behind for the first time when I traveled to Jamaica, because I needed some rest and relaxation after writing a book. They both said, "Oh, you're a writer?" to which I answered, "Not per se, but I just happened to finish writing my first book." I explained why I felt the need to write this book even though there have been many books written about race and adoption. I had recently read *P G County*, *Dreams from My Father*, and *The Book of Sarahs*—all with similar themes about race or adoption. Their stories, however, are not my story.

I explained that my goal was to help others who are struggling with the issues of being biracial, adopted, or not knowing where they belong—that I hoped to touch someone's spirit the way I have been touched by those who have shared their life stories with me.

I told the women that my name is Barbara. Or at least that is the name I have been called for most of my life. I'd been told that the name I was given at birth was Tanya. My adoptive mother told me that my birth mother was a 19-year-old, pretty, white woman who'd been attending college in New York, and that my birth father was a 21-year-old, very handsome, black man who'd been studying to be a physician.

As an adopted child, I wanted to know all about the intricacies of my birth that make me who I am. I wondered where I got my laugh, my smile, and even my desire to succeed. Who in my family shares my gift of gab, the cleft in my chin, my affectionate nature, or my very emotional side? I also wanted to know the many concrete pieces of information that most children know and take for granted, such as: Where was I born? How much did I weigh and what was my length? What was my mother's labor like? What time was I born? Did my mother ever hold me? Why was I given up for adoption? Are the date and location of my arrival on Earth documented correctly on my revised, adoptive birth certificate? For me, these were all mysteries that I longed to solve.

Not knowing the answers, I created scenarios in my mind. I imagined my biological parents in college, dating and in love. I supposed she got pregnant and her parents wouldn't allow her to keep me because I was black. It was the 1960s, a difficult time for people in mixed relationships. I often wondered if she really wanted to give me up or if she was just too young to go against her parents' wishes. I envisioned my birth father being very supportive of her during the entire pregnancy and birth. I accepted the notion that a child could hamper the aspirations of a medical student. Part of me hoped they stayed together and had more children. Other times I knew this was all a fantasy I had created, and my soul longed for the truth.

The questions I had about my birth and my parents would not necessarily be answered by seeing an original birth certificate. I have always been bothered by the fact that the government creates an altered, adoptive birth certificate for adopted children, to replace the names of the biological parents with the names of the adoptive parents. I have two such altered birth certificates. One has my race listed as white; the other lists it as black. When I lost the first one, I applied for the second. It seemed as if someone saw me at birth and assigned me to the white race and then whoever saw me later with darker skin assigned me to the black race. Another possibility is that someone assigned the race of my birth mother on the first birth certificate. I thought that if they could arbitrarily designate race on an official form, they might designate or even fabricate other birth information like the place of birth or even the date. In some cases, in fact, children are assigned the first or last day of their birth month as their official birthday.

It is only through another piece of paper that I learned a bit about who I was as a small child. It was a letter given to my new parents from my foster mother, Mrs. Bland, who cared for me shortly after my birth until I was adopted at 10 months of age.

It read:

"To Tanya's Mommy and Daddy

Tanya is a wonderful happy baby. She is very intelligent with a forward personality. She has an excellent appetite and sleeps very good. Tanya plays vigorously; because of her activeness you must strap her in everything such as her high chair or carriage—otherwise she'll stand up.

Tanya's sleeping habits vary. Sometimes she will take a morning and afternoon nap, sometimes only one nap a day. During her naptime and at night I never cover her because she likes to pull the blankets over her head. The safest thing, I would suggest for Tanya are blanket sleepers for winter. At night, also I would suggest for a while would be a night-light until she becomes familiar with her new home.

She loves cookies, lollypops and Jell-O, which I sometimes give between meals. She dislikes potatoes and junior meat. She loves Hamburg and chicken.

Tanya is now taking a few steps alone. I still keep her in the walker because with Tanya I think it is safer than crawling. I cannot think of anything else that might help but I would like you to feel free to call me anytime. I would like very much hearing from you. At the bottom of this letter I have written a schedule for Tanya's mealtime perhaps for a while you'd like to follow. I can add one very important thing. We all love Tanya very much and will miss her but I'm sure she will be happy and loved very much. Be very happy together and may God bless you all.

Sincerely yours, Mrs. Walter Bland

August 1964

That letter is all I know about the first year of my life. Most children hear many stories about their first year of life—their first smile, the first time they sat up, their first laugh, their first words, and unique characteristics that made them different from other children. Most children can visualize their infancy by looking at photographs and seeing how they changed as they grew.

With my own children, I took hundreds of pictures, wrote facts in baby books, and kept a journal for each of their first years in a book called *All About Me*. But I knew nothing about me. I didn't know what I looked like before the time I was nearly a year old. I was often sad that I didn't have any of those recorded memories. It was as if my first year didn't exist and no one remembered that time in my life.

The only thing I remember about Mrs. Bland is her spirit; I always thought of her as my guardian angel. I recall visiting her as an older child, right before my teen years, but the visits were few and far between. Mrs. Bland was quiet and sweet. She had a caring, gentle spirit. She adopted another child she was caring for, Angela, soon after my parents adopted me. I was told that she expected that Angela and I would both stay with her and be raised as sisters. When I was adopted, she adopted Angela so that Angela would always be with her. I have always wondered what my life would have been like if I had stayed with Mr. and Mrs. Bland and Angela. I would have had a sister.

As I grew older, I saw Angela occasionally. I called her my "almost sister." We looked like we could have been sisters. The last time I saw her, I was 30. We were both dating guys named Tony, who were friends. We hung out together and I was really happy to spend time with her. It was strange. We were never really sisters; we weren't related by blood. We were never close friends, but I was always happy to see her. I guess that was one of the many times I attached myself to someone based on my need for connection and belonging. When I was adopted, it was my first step toward belonging somewhere.

I went to live with my adoptive parents when I was 10 months old. My mother said I adjusted well and was a happy baby except that I was afraid of my father at first because he had a beard. The following is an entry from my mother's journal dated August 31, 1964.

> *"You hate your father, you refuse to have anything to do with him and he adores you. The two of you look at each other and he laughs at you. He thinks you are lovely and so do I ... (On another day she continues) ... while we were in the street you saw your daddy and yelled like a nut. Every time that he tries to hold you, you scream like you are afraid of him but there is never a tear in sight."*

Adoptive parents may try to convince themselves and their adopted children that children can become well adjusted having had two or three sets of parents, and several given names, early in life. When each of my children reached 10 months of age, I tried to imagine how they would feel if they were taken to a new home, with new parents, and given a new name. They were so attached to me, and me to them, at that age. I couldn't imagine it would not be traumatic for them. I also couldn't imagine that in some way, even if only in my subconscious, it wasn't also traumatic for me. Deep down I now know that until these issues are addressed, many of us have an empty place inside created by the circumstances of our birth. It wasn't until I started to read books about adoption that my feelings about that empty place were validated.

Nancy Verrier, author of *The Primal Wound*, says

> *The severing of that connection between the adopted child and his birthmother causes a primal or narcissistic wound, which affects the adoptee's sense of Self and often manifests in a sense of loss, basic mistrust, anxiety and depression,*

emotional and/or behavioral problems and difficulties in relationships with sig-nificant others.

She goes on to say that

The awareness, whether conscious or unconscious, that the original separation was the result of a "choice" made by the mother affects the adoptee's self-esteem and self-worth. Adoption, considered by many to be merely a concept, is, in fact, a traumatic experience for the adoptee ... he is wounded as a result of having suffered a devastating loss and thus his feelings about this are legiti-mate and need to be acknowledged, rather than ignored or challenged ... the mother/infant bond takes many forms and the communication between them is unconscious, instinctual, and intuitive ... The significance of that bond is con-firmed by the increasing numbers of adoptees and birthmothers who are out there searching for one another ... searching might be seen as an attempt to heal the primal wound about which there are no conscious thoughts, only feel-ings and somatic memories—and an aching sense of loss."

I am not implying that adoption is a bad thing. In fact, I think adoption is a great thing. I thank God I was adopted into a family where I was loved and nur-tured. I could have been aborted or could have spent years living in several foster homes. I always felt grateful for the sacrifice my birth mother made and never had any bad feelings toward her—only love and appreciation.

I loved my adoptive mother and father with all my heart and always felt they loved me, too. I also felt an empty place where my "birth family" belonged. This was probably exacerbated by the fact that I was raised as an only child by older parents. My mother said she'd wanted to adopt another child, but my father did not. For a long time I was angry about not growing up with a sibling.

My adoptive mother, Thelma, was a complex person. Short and beautiful, she swore, fought, and told dirty jokes. She was like a beautiful swan with a sailor inside. She also had a very strong, yet private, Catholic faith.

Thelma had a hard childhood. Her mother was a live-in maid, so her grand-mother raised her. She was teased and ashamed of her very light skin color—the result of the union between her black mother and her mother's white employer. She once told me that she was ashamed because she was a "bastard." She was rid-iculed because of her light skin and had to fight a lot because of all the teasing. She said they often called her "light, bright, and damn near white."

She left home and married early, got pregnant several times, but always miscarried. Once she almost reached full term, but the baby "died inside of her," which almost killed her, physically and emotionally. She said she was lucky to get through that alive. She divorced her husband and later remarried, moving to Massachusetts with her new, military husband. This husband cheated on her, getting another woman pregnant.

The light skin she was so ashamed of as a child helped her survive after the divorce. It was a lot easier to get a job as an "almost-white" woman. She told me that many of her relatives "passed" for white to survive the racism in the South. My mother said she wouldn't "pass" because she wouldn't deny her black heritage just to make it in society. She was, unlike me, unconcerned about what people thought of her.

My mother used to say that she was not only book-smart, but street-smart as well. She learned through life's hard knocks. She later met and married my adoptive father, despite bearing the stigma of being twice divorced. Her beauty and intelligence helped her overcome any obstacle in life—internal or external. To this day, I think my mom was the most beautiful and resilient woman I have ever known.

My mother often told me that my dad was the true love of her life. She wanted to have a child with him and was heartbroken when she couldn't. She became pregnant many times with him, but always miscarried. That is, of course, why I was adopted.

Back then, there was no effective counseling given to those desiring to adopt due to infertility. It must have been assumed that a "replacement child" would fix the problem for both the adoptee and the parents. I am not sure if parents in those days ever grieved their loss—their dream to have their own child—before adopting. I know that as an adopted child, I didn't get the support I needed.

Refusing to discuss difficult problems is never good, as it buries issues that need to be addressed. Because I looked so much like my adoptive parents, I used to say that I thought they had picked me out. But my mom later told me that since I didn't get a chance to check her out first, she didn't feel it was right to check me out first. She said she knew she would love a child no matter what he or she looked like or whether that child was a boy or girl. She did, however, later tell me she really wanted a son.

My mother was a loner. I realize now that she valued us, her small nuclear family, as much as I valued family. She also craved acceptance, despite saying that she didn't, and that is probably why we visited her friends and family even though they didn't visit us. We both had outward appearances that differed from our inner selves. I appeared happy and well adjusted, but was constantly seeking love, acceptance, and family. My mom had a gruff, hardened exterior that hid a lot of internal turmoil.

One tragedy that caused my mom a lot of pain involved her only sibling, her younger brother Elvin. Elvin was kind-hearted and very handsome, with striking green eyes. She often was required to look out for her brother—as his protector and caretaker. He served in the military, and when he left, he thought he would be treated with respect. My mom said he, like I, was very naïve. One day, he was driving down a country road when a group of white kids ran him off the road, killing him.

My mother said that young Elvin became just another statistic. He was one of countless black men killed at the hands of white men who would never be prosecuted for their crimes. My mother explained to me that it was hard to get a fair trial if you were black. She was very protective of Elvin but she said she couldn't protect him from a racist society.

She was also an overprotective parent who sometimes appeared harsh and overly strict despite having loving intentions. She was cynical and didn't trust many people. Some aspects of her personality were contradictory. She taught me to be distrustful of most white people, but at the same time, several of her closest friends were white. This was one of the many things I was confused and conflicted about during childhood.

I saw through that tough exterior of hers only a few times in her life. I saw her cry when my dad died and during the last year of her own life when she was depressed. When she got sick, it broke my heart to the point that it still hasn't healed. Both of these times were difficult for me. When she became a grandmother, however, she was joyful. With my children, she was the happiest I can remember seeing her. She became open, emotional, and loving.

My mother was such a tough person I thought she would live forever. She seemed able to survive anything. After her death I realized that I never really appreciated all the sacrifices she made for me. We spent many years not getting along because of her strictness. I now wish I could go back and relive the time that was wasted comparing her with "cool" moms of other teens or trying to fit into other people's families. I always knew she loved me, but we really didn't enjoy each other until the last few years of her life. She was very different than my adoptive father.

My Parents: Harold and Thelma Miller

Harold was a simple man, although not simple intellectually. In fact, he was very intelligent. He served in the Army and the Navy, was a truck driver, then took college courses and became a restaurant manager. He owned his own home prior to marrying my mom, which was rare for a black man in the 1950s. My mother thought he was the most handsome man she ever knew. He was dark-skinned and clean cut, and a man of few words. His nickname was Frog, which may have come from his reputation for being quiet, but likely to jump on anyone who messed with him.

My dad was not a warm person. I don't recall having many intimate conversations with him. I do, however, remember a few times when my mother would yell at me or chastise me for some offense I thought was trivial, and I would look at him for protection or support. He would simply say, "Don't get so upset about it, you know how your mother is." His words were brief, but on those few occasions, he looked at me as if he really understood what I was going through and, in his way, was being supportive.

What I saw of my father's life was rather predictable. He worked, came home, watched TV, fell asleep in his recliner, and then woke up in the middle of the night to go to bed. He always seemed to have a cigarette in his mouth or in his hand. He had friends he played golf with and socialized with on his weekly night out, but he didn't seem close to anyone but my mother. He occasionally attended school and church functions but I had the feeling he went under duress. His family members were Jehovah's Witnesses but he didn't attend meetings. When he said something nice or supportive to me, it was a big deal. Even though he seemed quiet and not demonstratively affectionate, he had a way with women and my mother was madly in love with him. Aside from my parents, I was blessed to have many other people in my life that loved me and helped me to feel like I belonged. One important person in my life was my godmother Claire, a white friend of my mother's. She was French and her husband was Polish. She was loving, caring, and warm, and treated me like I was special. Claire had a big family that was raised on a farm. She shared my love of animals and my emotional nature. I think we both felt that with animals, if you give them love, they will love you in return—just like little children.

I learned one of my greatest lessons from Claire and her family. That lesson was that love knows no color. When my mother yelled, hit, or criticized me, Claire reminded my mom of my good traits and that I was just a kid. It was as though my mom expected me to be perfect at all times; but no one is perfect. Claire was like family to me, which was especially helpful because I didn't have very many close relationships with my parents' families.

The few fond memories I have of my mother's extended family included trips to North Carolina during summer vacations. My mother and I rode a bus to the South for short visits to her family, some of whom still lived in the house where my mother was born. The house had a well and an outhouse in the backyard. We heated water for baths and used bedroom pots to go to the bathroom during the night. Some of the food we ate came from a large family garden. My brief visits to North Carolina were exciting adventures for me because of the sense of history and family. I was especially close with my older cousin Doris, who was like an older sister to me, and with my younger cousin Sonya. But even the unconditional love that these relatives showed me didn't fill my internal void, that need to belong.

Even though I loved the visits to North Carolina, I still longed for siblings and grandparents and the big family gatherings some other kids had. Most of the time, my family was my mother. I often felt very alone and secretly wished I could be a part of someone else's family. I realize now that is why I latched onto certain friends who would "adopt" me into their families.

Like most children, I don't remember too much about my life until after I was about 4 years old. My mother centered her life on me and worked at night while I was asleep so that she could be with me during my waking hours. One story in particular shows her doting attention to me. I was a toddler and I wanted her to take me for a walk. She was in the middle of baking a cake, but she stopped what she was doing and took me for the walk. She said that she always tried to make me happy and loved me more than anything in the world. I could tell by the way she looked at me in photographs that she adored me. She would dress me up and keep me as neat as a little doll.

I have only a few memories from before I was 4 years old, but I vaguely remember a tragic event that changed our lives forever. I can remember playing with two boys my mom babysat for, and I remember their mother, who I called "Bethel Mommy."

On the day I was christened, my mother and I were driving to see her close friend, Bethel, when I said, "There is daddy's car!" Mom was surprised because my father had said he couldn't attend my christening. My mother went to Bethel's house and was shocked to learn that my father and Bethel were more than just friends. My mother confronted my father and they got into a physical fight. Bethel got in the middle and suffered injuries that later took her life. I never asked, and was never told, exactly what caused her death. That one chance encounter, that tragic twist of fate, would haunt us all for years to come. It would be another secret, another separation, which I would have to come to terms with as an adult.

When I was older, some of her close friends told me the only reason my mother came back to my father after she'd spent a year-and-a-half in jail for causing Bethel's death was because of me. She thought it would be best for me to be raised with two parents. She wanted to give me a good life. Everything she did was for me. When I cried inconsolably when I visited her in prison, she told my father that as much as she wanted to see me, she didn't want me to be upset and would rather miss me than see me in so much pain.

During this time I went to live with my father's sister, Aunt Audrey. I remember not seeing my father often and only seeing my mother once for a little over a year. I was very sad and missed my mother desperately. The one time that I visited her, I recall that we were in a very white room and I felt terribly sad when I had to leave her and go back home with my aunt. I also remember the day that my aunt told me that my mom was coming home and how happy I was that I could be with her again.

For a long time I didn't understand why we were separated and was very confused. I got bits and pieces of the story over the years from my family and by reading letters my mother wrote to me while she was "away." The letters were heartbreaking to read when I got older because my mother kept telling me how much she loved me and kept saying that she hoped I wouldn't forget her and that she thought about me every day and couldn't wait to see me again.

As a little girl, I didn't understand why I didn't see my dad much during that time. I later learned that my father had another woman, who happened to be white, in our new home while my mom was gone. I am not sure if my father ever changed his ways, but I know that for many years there was a lot of arguing in the house. I was often afraid that I would lose the only family I knew if things didn't work out between my parents.

It wasn't until I became an adult that I understood the power and freedom that comes with forgiveness. It wasn't until then that I understood how the power of God's grace and mercy could give you the strength to get through life's trials and tribulations. I also understood the sacrifices my mother made for me and just how much inner strength and courage it took for her to rise above her mistakes and become a successful nurse, devoted wife, friend, and mother. I grew to realize that this was not something for me to be ashamed of—but rather a testimony about God's power in the lives of His believers.

I started kindergarten while living with my aunt. I recall being frightened one day when my cousin didn't come to walk me home. I decided to walk home alone. I was spanked for walking home alone but didn't understand why. My aunt told me that she was worried about me walking home alone at such a young age. As a child, I thought she was being mean. As an adult I realize how worried she must have been and what a sacrifice it was for her to care for me when my mother and father couldn't.

I went from living in a black neighborhood with my aunt and cousins to living in a predominantly white neighborhood with my parents. I didn't think I fit in anywhere. After coming home one day crying because a neighborhood child told me he didn't want to play with me because I was "brown," my mother explained to me that some of the white kids might call me "nigger" or reject me and not want to play with me because I was not white like them. She told me not to take it personally because they were just ignorant. Despite knowing I might face racism daily in this environment, my parents still thought that this neighborhood was the best place for us to live because it was safer than the inner city, and had better schools. Education was the most important thing to my mom. She said it was the key to success for a black person. My parents thought I would just "fit in." Outwardly, I did. I made friends in my neighborhood despite changing schools and being the new kid on the block. Inwardly, I did not.

My first best friend was Leslie, who lived a few houses away. Her family was the stereotypical all-American suburban family with many children. She had red hair and freckles and could not have been more different from me. I longed to be just like her. I mimicked her every move. I took dance lessons at a local dance studio. I joined the swim team. I took piano lessons like she did. However, there was one thing I could not mimic. I couldn't become white.

Leslie and I became friendly with another white girl whose name was Karna. She was very pretty, with blond hair. I dressed like they did in chinos and earth shoes, went to the parties they attended, and tried to copy their mannerisms in order to blend in.

As a child in the late 1960s, I wasn't aware of the racial tensions plaguing our society, but I was experiencing my own problems with racial identity. I knew I was mulatto, as we were labeled then, but I felt I couldn't talk about my racial background with my black adoptive parents. I thought my being adopted was a secret, not to be discussed. It felt like a constant stabbing wound in my heart knowing I may never know who my biological parents were and thus who I really was. My mother told me that Leslie and I wouldn't be lifelong friends because race affects relationships, as people get older. I was very angry with her for suggesting such a thing could happen, but of course, she was right. We didn't remain lifelong friends.

My mother's awareness about issues of race and discrimination also affected her relationships with her other family members. My Aunt Annie worked as a live-in maid for a white family. She looked very much like my mother, with very light skin and thin, black hair. Aunt Annie worked hard and the family she worked for treated her well; she often said that she felt like a member of their family.

One day I walked in on a conversation my mom was having with Aunt Annie. I could hear Aunt Annie speaking in her sweet soft voice saying, "The family I take care of treats me nice. I know they really care about me."

"Annie, when are you going to wake up and realize those white folks may seem nice to you but you're just their servant girl, nothing more, nothing less."

"Thelma, you don't know them like I know them. Just because I work for them doesn't mean they don't care about me. They said as long as I live, they'd make sure I am taken care of."

"I guess we will just have to wait and find out about that won't we," my mother said.

I was upset because I could tell my mother was hurting my Aunt Annie's feelings. I walked in and said, "Mommy, why are you being mean to Aunt Annie?"

"Barbie, you need to be quiet," she said. "I told you about getting into grown folks' business." She paused and began to walk out of the room. Then she continued, "You and your Aunt Annie are just as naïve as Elvin."

Aunt Annie was the sweetest, kindest, gentlest person I knew and it hurt me to hear my mother talk to her that way—just as it hurt me when she told me that my closest friends wouldn't be in my life forever. She said that many white people don't like black people and that everyone isn't as loving and accepting as her close friends, such as my godmother Claire. This made me realize that Anais Nin was correct that "we don't see things as they are, we see them as we are."

During the early 1970s, I began hearing comments that became old tapes played over and over in my head. "You're not like other black kids." "You are prettier than most black kids." "You are smarter than other black kids." "You can't be all black because you are so pretty and have such *good* hair." At the time, I thought they were compliments (and maybe they were intended to be from the perspective of my equally naive young friends). I was just happy to be accepted. As I got older, those comments shaped my self-worth and my opinions about my people. If I thought someone was prejudiced against black people, I avoided talking about my racial identity so that I could fit in. On one occasion, when I visited another friend, Jeannie, her mother mistook me for an Italian girl. I realized that I could blend into many environments and that racial identity wasn't always as clear-cut as black and white.

Another comment that became one of the tapes in my head was that as a black girl, I would have to do everything better than my white friends to be on the same playing field. My mom frequently told me this. And because of it, I strove for greatness in every endeavor. I loved learning and loved to show how smart I was in class by answering questions faster than other students. Other kids dreaded getting report cards. I loved it. My academic achievements gave me a reason to feel good about myself.

In spite of the fact that I was succeeding academically, always with As and Bs, I had buried another incident deep inside my unconscious. It probably had an effect on my self-worth and self-esteem. It involved the son of one of my mother's friends, Auntie Sweety. She was an adopted white woman born in England. She was another special person in my life who taught me that true love is colorblind. Because I was an only child, I tagged along with my mom to visit her friends. I sat at Auntie Sweety's table sipping tea and listening to adult conversations. I never asked questions or spoke as I was told kids are to be seen and not heard when adults are talking. I learned about cheating husbands, how to catch a bargain, and the workings of their adult world. I also got to hang around Chrissy, Aunt Sweety's daughter, who was like an older sister to me. Unfortunately, when Chrissy wasn't at home, I was expected to hang out with her older brother, who had cerebral palsy.

It wasn't until I was a 21-year-old nursing student learning about child sexual abuse that I recalled several traumatic events. I guess a child's mind only allows a certain amount of information to be processed at a time. As an adult, when I remembered the times Chrissy's brother tried to touch me in private places, I felt weak and vulnerable just like I did when it happened. At that time I was still in elementary school and afraid to talk to my mother about anything. When I recalled these events as an adult, even though I felt more comfortable talking to my mother about important issues, I was afraid to tell her what Chrissy's brother had done to me because I feared she would cause him physical harm and then she would be out of my life again. I also didn't want to destroy her long-time, close friendship with Auntie Sweety, whom I loved dearly. I was always worried about keeping the peace and not destroying relationships. That would continue throughout my childhood and adult years, along with my need for acceptance.

In my quest for acceptance, I tried to be a great swimmer like my friends. I joined the Sharks Swim Team. I practiced regularly and carpooled with the other kids. Their parents were very involved in the team. Karna's dad wrote articles for the community paper about the team. My photo was in the paper but the inscription under the photo had the name of the other black girl on the team who didn't look anything like me. I thought to myself, "Can't they even tell us apart or do they really think all black kids look alike?"

I had conflicted feelings about my parents not coming to my swim meets and not being as involved with the team as the other parents. On one hand I thought they didn't care about me. On the other hand, it was easier for me to blend into my friends' little circle without my parents around, as they didn't look or act like the other parents did.

My involvement with the swim team also made me painfully aware of the difference in economic status between my teammates and me. I'd always thought we had as much money as anyone else until I joined the Sharks. We couldn't afford a team swimsuit so I had to wear a second-hand green wool swimsuit that was purchased at one of my mother's favorite stores, Goodwill, which she affectionately called "Goodies." Everyone teased me about that ugly green swimsuit. My self-esteem sunk even lower. Not only was I one of only two black kids on the team, and not the best swimmer, but also I had to wear a swimsuit that was an eyesore. Karna's father said the team would buy me a team swimsuit, which only made me feel like a charity case.

Still, I was determined to strive for excellence. I practiced diligently for four years and attained one of my most important goals: I became a member of one of the top relay teams and gained the same recognition as the most renowned swimmers. I also swam the individual 100-yard butterfly in every one of the meets.

My friends were also members of a private swim club called Bass Pond. My mother let me join that swim club so that I could hang out with my friends during the summer. I was the only black member. My skin turned dark brown while theirs darkened to my usual color, making our difference more evident. I later learned to love my brown tanned skin, but back then, I didn't. I just wanted to blend in.

It is hard to look back at the extent of my self-hatred. Not only did my skin not tan the same way that my teammates' skin tanned, but also the water in the pond wrought havoc on my hair and my body was not built like theirs. I had thick hair, thick thighs, and a big butt to boot. Instead of appreciating the things that made me unique, I hated them. Thank God I love them now.

Despite my parents' lack of involvement in my swim meets, my mother did attend a meet at Bass Pond, near the end of my swim career. I was excited at the opportunity to show her what a great swimmer I had become. I received several trophies that day, but there was one that was most precious. I competed against my friend Leslie, who was always a better swimmer than I. I beat her and it made me feel that in some small way I was as good as she was. It is peculiar how things can be of utmost importance at one time in a person's life and become totally insignificant later on. I was proud of myself that day and felt like I really belonged. Then things began to change.

When I was in the sixth grade, in 1974, busing was instituted in my hometown of Springfield. My mother was angry because she and my father had bought the house in the suburbs so that I could attend the schools in that neighborhood. I was bused to a school in another neighborhood with more black kids. I liked the fact that there were more kids who looked like me, but to them I acted "too white." I was confused again. I was happy with this new school and excited about being in a place where I felt more comfortable, but I began to think, "How do I fit in here?"

PART II
Finding Myself

2

Where Do I Fit in?

Fate chooses our relatives. We choose our friends.

—*Jacques Boussuet*

I sometimes wonder how anyone survives the teen years, what with the untrust-worthy friends, raging hormones, dating dramas, and school pressures that per-meate that time. We appear carefree and happy on the outside, but many of us are dying on the inside. Teens who came from families that I called "normal" were not exempt. With all of my baggage, I am amazed I made it through those years. The two adages that come to mind are: "God doesn't give you more than you can handle" and "What doesn't kill you, makes you stronger." I believe these to be the reasons my mother and I each survived the drama in our lives.

My mother said that I began to change when I entered Junior High School in 1975. Most of the kids I knew were also changing. Their bodies were maturing physically, while every fiber of my being was changing except my physical body. I didn't develop as quickly as my girlfriends, although I felt the change in my hor-mones. My new friend Sandi, a very pretty and popular black girl I met in fifth grade, began to look like a teenager. I was still stuck in the body of a little girl, with a ponytail on either side of her head.

When I started Kiley Junior High School, I hung out exclusively with my white friends and behaved as I always had. I did only the things that interested them, like playing the violin and swimming. Some of them tried smoking, so I tried smoking. Luckily, I didn't like it. Most of them did well in school and so did I. At the same time, I began to meet black kids. I discovered that black people and white people had different preferences.

I found black boys and black music very appealing. I discovered that WHYN, the only station I heard on the radio at home, which played top 40 and pop old-

21

ies, wasn't the only radio station in town. I turned off David Cassidy and the Partridge Family and turned on The Jackson 5 and Foster Sylvers. I yearned to find a way to fit into black culture, but didn't know how. My parents couldn't help. They were black, but much older than my friends' parents. They said, "Just be yourself," but "myself" was lost between two worlds.

Luckily, I had "Aunt Dot"—a former babysitter I visited from time to time. She had a house full of kids who knew all the new dances, such as "The Freak," and knew where the black kids went. I learned about the Girls Club, the Hill Jets Club, the Dunbar Community Center, and all the places where black kids socialized. Aunt Dot's kids and my friend Sandi were a godsend to me at this point in my life. They probably never realized how important they were to me.

Over the next three years, I adapted to having white friends and black friends. Junior High School is the time when most kids want to learn to be "cool." Even though I had a few black friends like Bea, Cheryl and Velada who didn't care if I was cool, I still wanted to be with the in crowd. One of the things the cool kids did was swear a lot. I had no problem picking up that skill. In spite of my mother's demonstration of grace, tact, and class, she also knew how to swear like a sailor. So I followed her lead.

I also became more defiant. Some of my new black friends weren't taking upper-level, more-advanced classes, so I didn't want to take those, either. I wanted to be in the classes they were in. But, thank God, my mom stressed the importance of good grades. I did all of my fooling around with my classmates in homeroom because that grade didn't matter. I never let go of my desire to succeed in my education.

It was at Kiley Junior High School that I met my new best friend, Micki. Micki had typical mulatto features and the guys found her light skin and "good" hair attractive. She had a bubbly, outgoing personality like mine. We both had a very silly side that kept us laughing most of the time we were together. Micki's mom was white and her dad was black. She lived with her mom. I felt comfortable with her and her brothers. They lived in a black neighborhood, which was where I longed to be.

Micki's mom was a "cool mom"—something I'd always wished I had. She was young; she listened to our music and was more lenient. The children weren't as pressured to get excellent grades. They were able to smoke, hang out, and didn't get whipped the way I did. Instead, Micki's mom would talk to them and give them a punishment such as writing a paper about what they did wrong and what they learned from it. Micki was able to talk to her mother about boys and anything else that was on her mind. I grew to wish they were my family. When I threatened to run away from home, she offered to take me in. Even though I never did run away, it meant a lot to me to know I would have a place to go. Micki's mother made me fantasize about my own biological mother. I looked at every young, white woman I saw and wondered if she was my biological mother.

I had another friend, Toni, who lived in the housing projects. She was cute, light-skinned, popular, and "cool." I also wanted to be just like her. She skipped school, smoked weed, had boyfriends, and could stay out until midnight if she wanted. I had to be home when the streetlights came on. I didn't realize how troubled Toni was. She was very tough. She got into a lot of fights and had a lot of drama in her life. She told me if anyone messed with me she would take care of him or her for me. She began to shoplift and supposedly joined a gang. My mother forbade me to see her, but of course that made me want to see her even more.

Once, I told my parents that I was riding my bike to a local park and instead rode to Toni's house across town. One of my mother's friends saw me and called my house. My father was so angry; he spanked me for the first time in my life. My parents made strange remarks like "Don't you know the boys in those projects could have run a train on you?" I had no idea they were talking about gang rape.

My mother was puzzled by my hysteria. She didn't understand that Toni's friendship meant a lot to me. We were so close that my mother accused me of having a homosexual relationship with her, which was far from the truth. I thought perhaps my mom had a warped mind. I later realized that my mother was so fearful of any negative influences in my life that she overreacted when trying to protect me. She never wanted me to learn lessons the hard way, as she had.

My high school years were both a great time and a depressing time in my life. Like most teens, hormones raged, friends changed, and one's outlook on life changed as well. For me it was no different. When time came to choose a high school, my goal was to go where the black kids went. Most of the white kids went to Classical High School, a college prep school. That was not my choice even though I wanted to go to college. I wanted to show off the new "real me" in a more diverse environment. My mother, who was always in survival mode, allowed me to enroll in the High School of Commerce because it offered college prep courses as well as typing and stenography so that I could land a job while in college, if I needed one. This choice was agreeable to me, as it was a place where I could be exposed to more black students.

I remember getting one of my most severe punishments when I was in the tenth grade. Some of my friends invited me to skip school with them. I was more concerned with being ridiculed by my new friends than I was of being caught, so I went along with then. We went to a friend's house, where we all started smoking weed. I got very paranoid and decided to get out of there. When I caught the bus back to school at lunchtime, I found out that the school had already called my mother and she was on her way to the school. I wanted to die! No one else got caught because they were often absent. It was an oddity for me to ever miss a class. I thought, "If I am an A student, what's the big deal if I miss a few classes?"

It was a big deal. I received a whipping I would never forget. I was put on punishment for three months with no contact by phone or visitation with any of my friends. The next day, I went to school and my gym teacher saw my bruises. When I told my mother that I told my gym teacher how I got them, my mother's response was, "So what?" She went on to say that they could put me in a foster home. As unhappy as I was in that strict environment, I could not envision losing the only family I had ever known. I never told her that I had actually lied to my gym teacher to cover up what really happened. I never tried anything like that again.

A few months later I overheard that my so-called friend Toni found my punishment amusing. That taught me a valuable lesson about doing things to get approval from people who don't really care about me.

My friends considered me a good girl with strict parents. It seemed like I was always on punishment for some minor infractions like talking back or coming in after the streetlights went on or lying to spend time with my friends—all things that most kids did without major retribution. My constant punishments became a running joke, and my friends—and later on my boyfriends—would ask "are you still on punishment?" before inviting me anywhere.

My rescuers were Micki and Sandi and Aunt Dot. Those were fun-filled homes. When I was there, I could experience typical teen life. Other than those few places, my mother portrayed the world as dangerous, with many bad influences. It probably was that way, but I didn't see it. I wondered why, if the world were so dangerous, I was allowed to do things like riding buses alone to meet her at work or stay at home alone when I was in the second grade, but was unable to hang out with my friends when I reached high-school age. I guess it was one of those contradictions about my mother that remained a mystery to me. I think maybe, in her opinion, it was a matter of necessity versus frivolity.

I am now very grateful to my mother for not letting me do the things I wanted to do with my so-called friends during my teen years. Many of them became unwed teen mothers, drug addicts, or went to jail. Bad boys intrigued me, but I wasn't allowed to date them. What seemed like a curse then I now realize was a blessing.

I am also grateful for the people who were a positive influence at that time in my life. They included the Akers, a black family who lived around the corner. Their mother's name was the same as mine, Barbara. She treated me like one of her kids. Mike and Michelle (her twins) were good, church-going, respectful kids. They were raised under a set of rules similar to those in my family. We used to joke about all of the times we were punished for not getting home before the streetlights came on. As time went on, we learned how to time our race home based on whose house we were at to avoid our parents' wrath. We went to different high schools but always remained friends. My mother wished that I would date Michael, but we were just great friends. The Akers supported and accepted me. Little did I know then that they would remain in my life, sharing my adult discoveries and my spiritual growth.

The first "good guy" that I fell for I met when we were both in the tenth grade. His name was Tommy. A mutual friend named Melonie introduced us. He was a light-skinned black boy with red hair. I thought he was cute and I heard he came from a good family. He had more freedom than I did but his parents still kept a close watch on his comings and goings. We spent a lot of time together going to parties, the mall, and visiting each other at home. He wrote me poems and letters and gave me sweet gifts. I liked his family and my family liked him. Tommy and I grew so close that his father said we were "way too serious" for high school and after only four months we had to break up. I was heartbroken. In hindsight, of course, his father was right. We did, however, remain close friends throughout our adult years. I know now that heartbreak is a rite of passage that many teens must endure. It is also an experience I learned to survive over and over again.

When Tommy and I broke up in the tenth grade, my mother and my Auntie Sweety wiped away my tears. My mother had a rule that I could only talk on the phone between 6 and 7 PM. Tommy called that night to explain why he had to write the break-up letter and to make sure I was OK. I wasn't allowed to talk to him because it was after 7 PM. My mother snatched the phone out of my hand and I reacted in a way that made us both think I had lost my mind.

Most girls were looking for cute guys who could provide fun. I was searching for true love and marriage. I didn't want to waste time on adventure. All my life, I have been more interested in loyalty, love, and commitment than a good time. It is too bad I didn't realize then that I was too young to be so serious. I didn't want to have to get to know and trust new people. I preferred to stay with untrustworthy friends or boyfriends and try to find some good in them rather than meeting new people. I have been loyal to many people who didn't deserve it. I was much too trusting. It was sad that the need for love and acceptance prevented me from making good decisions.

During my junior year in high school in 1979, I was doing well academically, was popular, and became a cheerleader. I got a job on a tobacco farm over the summer and was able to buy all the clothes I wanted. I was excited about dating again. I was feeling like I could see the end of my high school years. I began to feel that I fit in, despite still not liking everything about myself. I thought my skin was too light, my butt was too big, and that I was too thick wearing my size 7 pants. It is amazing how many teens have poor self-esteem because they compare themselves with what the media calls beautiful.

In my junior year, I started dating Pete, another popular guy from the 'hood. He was yet another boy with light skin I thought was cute. Toni introduced us. Pete was younger than me but I liked that. My mother said that the younger boys didn't "want" as much as the older ones—or so she thought.

I got very close to Pete's family. His sister Peaches went to my school. His sister Marcia introduced me to reggae music and Bob Marley. Another sister, Holly, was rough and tough and said she'd always have my back if anyone bothered me. Every year, I had a different girl who threatened to scratch up my face or hurt me because "I thought I was cute." Little did they know, I didn't feel cute at all.

I could talk to Pete's mother about anything. His dad was genuinely nice and talked to me—something my own dad rarely did. When we grew apart after dating for almost a year, I was more upset about losing his family than losing him. I think my mom was happy when it happened.

She thought I should be trying to date guys who were more like the type she wanted me to marry. She always said I should try to "marry up" not "marry down." She wanted me to meet an educated man or one from a well-to-do family, not a poor boy from the projects who didn't plan to go to college. During that time, with the introduction of hip-hop music, I was more intrigued by guys from the 'hood than nice guys from the suburbs. But that was about to change.

In my senior year, I dated the first real love of my life. I believed what I had experienced before was "puppy love," but this was the real thing. Greg was tall and handsome, with the most hypnotizing light-brown eyes I had ever seen. He was popular. He showered me with gifts, love, and attention. His family, which ran a successful business, loved me. He was the first person I seriously dated who was older, and he was mature for his age. We became engaged when I was still in high school after dating for only six months. I thought I had found my prince charming.

During this year, I finally felt like my life was about to be perfect. I was comfortable in my own skin, my parents gave me a little more freedom, and I was able to drive. I had a job and my future looked bright.

My mother approved of my relationship with Greg. She thought he was a nice guy despite his being older than I. He picked me up after school in his sister's sporty car and took me to Burger King where all the kids hung out. He had a job and he made me feel like a princess. I spent a lot of time at his house where we were allowed alone time in his room. We listened to Teddy Pendergrass singing *Turn Off the Lights* and Peabo Bryson singing *Feel the Fire*. This was something that could never have happened at my house, where my mother always found a reason to come into the den or basement so she could see what my friends and I were doing.

Because we had a lot of privacy at Greg's house, I began to feel more like a woman than a girl. We were inseparable. We went to parties and concerts. Once we modeled in a fashion show together. When we got engaged, my father said I couldn't wear the ring on my finger because I was too young, but I could wear it around my neck. I am sure he knew that I took it off the chain and put it back on my finger every day to show the world I was engaged. Once again, it all seemed picture perfect.

As my work and school schedule became busier, I had less time on weekdays to spend with Greg. On weekends, he worked late in the evenings as a DJ. I couldn't stay with him because of my curfew. I was afraid we were growing apart. I began feeling more insecure and developed a terrible trait, jealousy. I never wanted to live without him, and many pretty, popular girls liked him. He was a big flirt, although he always treated me with respect when we were together. He continually reassured me that he loved me and we'd live happily ever after, and I believed him. I also began trying to figure out what other things I believed.

I began my spiritual journey during my middle-and high-school years. My mother was raised Roman Catholic but she didn't attend church because she had been excommunicated when she divorced. However, she wanted me to be raised in the same faith. My father's family was Jehovah's Witnesses but he didn't attend church, either. I rode my bike almost three miles every Sunday to attend church alone. I tried to be a good Catholic girl by attending church and youth classes, but I never really experienced true faith. I went through the ritualistic Masses and learned morality and the difference between right and wrong, but not the deep faith I desired.

When I watched a movie about the story of Jim Jones and his followers, who committed mass suicide in Guyana as an expression of their faith, I was absorbed by it. I initially thought he was a great white man who really cared about black people. Instead I learned about how power can corrupt. I wished for faith so deep that I would go to such lengths to serve God and it frightened me so that I couldn't sleep. I talked to my mom and she comforted me and told me to call my priest. All he could offer was, "Your faith is weak. You need to spend more time in church." I already attended regularly and his words gave me no comfort.

It also scared me that I had doubts about salvation and heaven because I couldn't find proof of these things. From the time I was in high school, I church hopped with many of my friends, but it wasn't until I was 38 years old that I found the faith that I had been searching for at St. John's Congregational Church in Springfield. I feel God called me to this church. The Bible-based teaching, preaching, and fellowship has changed my life and helped me find my "real family." I finally stopped attending Catholic Church when I was a senior in high school.

Many things in life, like religion, can be taught; but in order for them to be real to us as individuals they have to be felt. That is how I feel about my faith in God. I learned about God when I was young, but I didn't feel it in a way that it transformed my life until I became an adult. I am thankful that my mother exposed me to her faith, which I feel opened the door for me to find my own personal relationship with God.

I think my mother tried to help me gain wisdom and learn many of life lessons not only by exposing me to things she felt were important like church but also to people who could help me gain insight in a way that she could not. She didn't want me to have to learn about everything by experiencing it, so she occasionally allowed me to have relationships with people who were street smart and would look out for me. One such person was an older adopted girl in my neighborhood named Lynn.

Lynn was Greek. She had beautiful olive skin and long, black hair—she was absolutely gorgeous, and four year older than I. She was involved in a lot of extra-curricular activities and was very popular. She studied dance with Frank Hatchet who later left Springfield to become a choreographer on Broadway. Her adoptive parents were both black. My mother let me associate with her and my friend Sandi despite the fact that they did things I wasn't allowed to do. She probably knew that they would protect me and respect her wishes, and would not to try to influence me to do certain things.

I was fascinated with Lynn for several reasons. She was pretty, popular, and we identified with each other because of our biracial looks and adoptive parents. We could talk about anything. She called herself my big sister, since neither of us had a sister.

As Lynn got older, it became obvious that she was destined to go to New York City to be a model. She felt she could never fit into "the Springfield mentality." It may have been the punk influence that caused her to dye her bangs blue and dress differently. She was definitely her own person, cut from a different mold. I envied this about her, as I was always so busy trying to blend into my environment rather than trying to just be myself. It amazed me that her conservative, religious parents didn't go crazy watching some of her antics.

To my surprise, one day in my senior year of high school, my "sister" Lynn called me to the office for early dismissal. Since the school didn't put early dismissals on report cards, I decided to take a chance and leave with her. I was overjoyed at the thought of an adventure with Lynn. She said she wanted me to meet her boyfriend and his sister, whom she worked with. I didn't know where she worked but I was curious to find out. We pulled into the parking lot of a club and entered through the darkness where music was playing. As my eyes became accustomed to the darkness, we met her boyfriend, who escorted us to seats at the bar. His sister walked toward us on top of the bar. I am still amazed that I was able to speak a coherent word when this topless woman bent down and shook my hand. This was the first of many surprising things I was to learn about Lynn.

It is said that experience is the best teacher. Wisdom can be attained, however, through someone else's experiences, which, in many cases, can save the pain of gaining firsthand knowledge. One of the valuable lessons I learned from Lynn was to keep an open mind about people. She taught me to accept people who are different and not to judge a book by its cover. Sexual orientation, alternative lifestyles, blue hair, or dreadlocks do not make up all there is about a person. Other lessons I learned without firsthand experience were about the dangers of drug use and the drama of relationships. My relationship with Lynn taught me what it was like to have a sister who would love and protect me. We shared adoption backgrounds but we were different in most other ways. She was strong-willed and daring, even fearless. She moved to New York City and pursued her modeling career while working odd jobs to survive—and survive she did. She was once featured in a full-page photo spread in one of the New York City newspapers.

I may not have been as fearless and Lynn but I was always determined to succeed in my education. As time for graduation came closer and it was time to pick a college, Greg and his family suggested Rutgers University. It was a good school with several campuses. His family was originally from Scotch Plains, New Jersey. They had a beautiful home there where we could live after we were married. His sister was also getting married and was planning to move back to New Jersey. I didn't care where we lived, as long as we could be together. He promised to come to visit me every weekend until his entire family moved back to New Jersey.

My mother wanted me to attend Cornell University in upstate New York. She knew that I would be accepted because I was an A student with high SAT scores. She said she had connections there that could provide scholarship money. I could not see myself living back in a predominantly white environment away from the love of my life. She let me make the choice, but if I went to Rutgers, the only thing she would do for me was give me the four thousand dollars she had saved. Beyond that, I'd be on my own. I chose Rutgers. I thought I could manage to make it through college with my own savings and what she would give me.

I don't think I can fully describe how excited I was during my last days in high school. I loved my classes, enjoyed being a cheerleader, finally felt accepted by my peers, and was about to graduate at the top of my senior class. I was on top of the world. My parents were still a little strict. They made me come home from my senior prom by midnight to avoid what usually happens on prom night. They didn't know that what they feared had already happened. I could look forward to the restrictions and rules being over when I went away to college.

After my picture appeared in the newspaper for being class valedictorian, several of my friends told me that their parents said they would have given them a car, a big graduation party, or a trip somewhere if they had done as well as I did in school. They wanted to know what I was getting for a graduation gift. I told them that I wasn't having a big party but instead a small family gathering at my house. I told them I didn't know if I would get a graduation gift but I did know that I wasn't getting a car or any other extravagant gift because I knew that my parents wouldn't use the money they did have for something that they felt I should save up and pay for myself. College was the priority for them. All of this talk about big gifts and how proud other parents would be if their children succeeded academically as I did made me wonder about how my parents felt. I don't remember my dad ever saying he was proud of me although my mom said that he was. Since we never really had intimate conversations, I didn't bother to talk to him about my feelings.

We had a small family gathering at our home that included some of my dad's family and a few of my friends. My mom baked a graduation cake for me and prepared some of her best home-cooked foods. My parents gave me a graduation gift of five hundred dollars that was to be used for college. I was happy about all of the effort my mother made to celebrate my graduation but did feel a little let down that she didn't make a big deal of my senior-year straight A's or my graduating first in the class. I said, "Mommy, I know you said that daddy was proud of me, but are *you* really proud of me?"

"Of course I am proud of you Barbie!" she replied, and then paused. "I always expected you to be the best. I knew you had it in you all along. You always were book smart. You just were never very street smart."

I thought to myself, "What does my not being very street smart have to do with today?"

Then she said, "I am more proud of the fact that you got through high school without getting on drugs or becoming pregnant."

Knowing my mom the way I did, I shouldn't have been surprised by her response.

3

Loving the Skin You're in

This above all: To thine own self be true.

—*William Shakespeare*

I entered Rutgers University in the fall of 1981. I was bubbling with excitement about taking college classes and being on my own. In spite of all of my insecurities, I wasn't afraid of being alone. I met a girl named Julie at a Rutgers's summer honors program. We seemed very compatible and even had the same birthday. I felt like I was all set, especially since I wasn't the type of person who needed a lot of friends—just one good friend was enough for me. I thought she'd fit the bill.

I entered college not knowing exactly what I wanted to study. When I was younger, I wanted to be a veterinarian. During high school, I thought I wanted to be a pediatrician. I loved kids for the same reasons I loved animals—both respond to others without regard to race or class. They respond only to how they are treated. Later, after reading Jane Goodall's, *In the Shadow of Man*, my fascination with primates (especially chimpanzees) grew, and I thought about moving to Africa to study them. I knew I would figure out what to do with my life and my career once I "found myself" in college. Academics were something that I could master. In my senior year of high school, I shared the honor of being voted "most likely to succeed" with Dominic Sarno, who is currently an elected city official in Springfield, and Anna Guarna, our class president. I always believed I would be a success in whatever career I chose.

I loved the diversity of the Rutgers campus. I felt I could leave my past behind and show people only the parts of me I wanted to reveal. No one had to know my struggles with race and identity. No one had to know about my sheltered life and strict parents, or any of the skeletons in my closet. But I learned to understand the saying "Wherever you go, there you are." The "me" from home was the same "me" at college. The same old issues began to resurface.

I didn't fit in with my new roommate Julie. She was from the Washington, DC area and was more of a partier than I was. There were often people in our room, making a lot of noise and using my things. As an only child I wasn't used to that kind of sharing, and they interrupted my studying. We weren't roommates for long, but we parted with no hard feelings.

My new roommate Michelle and I had a lot in common. We were only children, we majored in biology, and we came from sheltered homes with strict mothers. She also had a mixed heritage. Her father was Hispanic and her mother was Jamaican. She, unlike me, embraced both of her ancestral cultures—probably because she was raised with their influence. She had a shape like mine and was very pretty. She was meticulous about her personal grooming. Her nails were always manicured and she spent a lot of time keeping her thick hair lustrous and in the latest styles. I don't ever remember seeing her having a bad hair day.

Michelle was also different from me in many ways. I loved listening to slow jams or artists with the Minneapolis Sound such as Prince, The Time, Vanity 6, and Sheila E. She, on the other hand, enjoyed listening to jazz while she studied. She was more shy and quiet, which is very different from my talkative, outgoing nature. With those who knew her well, however, she was open and silly, with an infectious laugh.

Michelle became my best friend. We shared classes, meals, and all of our free time. I was able to talk to her without fear or feelings of insecurity. She cared about me in spite of my problems. I felt accepted, and for the first time in a long time, I felt it was OK to just be me and be true to myself.

When I arrived on campus, one of my favorite things to do was take a late night ride on the campus bus. I rode around campus going nowhere in particular, listening to Peabo Bryson, my favorite singer at the time, on my Walkman radio. I was thrilled riding around, taking in the sights without a curfew. I was making up for all the things I thought I had missed when I lived at home. I enjoyed the simple things like the cafeteria with all of its fast food, desserts, and sweetened cereal. These were normal things to other kids but they were new and exciting for me.

My first semester was great. Greg visited every weekend. We stayed in his parent's home in Scotch Plains while preparing for his sister's wedding where I was to be a bridesmaid. We spent a lot of time at arcades playing Pac-Man, going to movies and dance clubs, and seeing all of the sights in New Jersey.

His cousin was dating Joy, who was involved in the music business. We were guests at Studio 54 one night when Aura, the group that sang *Are you single?* was performing. Starlena, the lead singer, gave me an outfit to wear so I could fit into the New York City scene. I was excited to see and do things I'd never experienced at home.

During this semester, I took a class called The Black Experience in America. It changed my perspective on race and America forever. I learned about black history and black leaders I had never heard of before. I was fascinated as a young child when I first saw *Roots*, but this course was even more fascinating. My professor was a down-to-earth guy named Professor Wilson. He taught us about apartheid in South Africa, as well as many other struggles people of color were enduring that were never mentioned in my high-school history classes. He took the class to the Schaumburg Museum in New York City. The exhibits of shackles that slaves had to wear and their original bills of sale horrified me and forever changed how I viewed the struggles our people suffered. Being called nigger took on new meaning for me. I also understood the rage my mother felt at being called that name.

At the same time, I developed a deepening black pride after learning about the many accomplishments of my people and the suffering they endured in paving the way for me to have the opportunity to vote, attend college, live in a nice home, and achieve success. I was also very angry with the generations of white people who tormented and terrorized my people. At the same time, I became ashamed of my early childhood when I wanted to be like my white friends and didn't want to talk about my black heritage. The course gave me such a thirst for knowledge in African-American studies that even after two semesters of Black Experience in America, I wasn't fulfilled. I dedicated my sophomore year's independent study class to learn more about The Black Experience with Professor Wilson, who became one of my favorite professors at Rutgers.

At the end of my first semester, I looked forward to going home for a month and spending time with Greg. But when I got home, I noticed that his behavior had changed. I heard a rumor he was seeing someone else, someone that I knew well. I couldn't believe she would date Greg knowing that we were engaged. I also never thought he would cheat on me. I was obviously naïve and in denial.

One night after hearing that Greg was at this girl's house, I gathered up the fortitude (or stupidity) to knock on her door. She answered and said Greg was there. He said they were just friends, but I knew in my heart they were more. Needless to say, I broke up with him and called off our engagement. I was humiliated and devastated. That month home, without Greg, was one of the hardest times of my young life. It was also one of the few times I felt close to my father. He offered to drive me to Greg's house to return the ring. That small gesture let me know that he supported my decision and me. That month, I stayed up late every night with my father, falling asleep to Hawaii 5-0. He fell asleep in his chair in the den and I stayed up until I could no longer keep my eyes open to avoid crying myself to sleep.

When I returned to school, I felt more alone than ever. My mother reminded me that it was a bad idea for me to choose a school because it was where my fiancé's family lived. If it weren't for my roommate Michelle, I probably would have lost my mind. I never thought of a future that didn't include Greg. I had to start thinking of the positive things in my life. I focused on the fact that I was free of parental restrictions and could do anything I wanted. It was hard to maintain friendships with my male friends while I was engaged. Now I could get reacquainted with them. I would also have more time to hang out with Michelle, although she often went home on weekends.

One weekend when she didn't go home, we attended a concert at the Rutgers Athletic Center that featured Peabo Bryson and Phyllis Hyman. I attended many concerts during high school. Groups came to the Civic Center every couple of months. But, for me, this was special because Peabo was singing. We were even invited to meet him and attend an after party. We met Peabo's brother, who took us out to eat after we'd met my favorite singer. Many people in the music business were there and we even ran into Greg's friend Joy while we were in Newark. That night was one of the best I had ever spent in college.

When Michelle was not around, I met other friends, including Darlene—another light-skinned, big-butt girl like Michelle and me. The three of us were often called "the butt sisters" after that old song about Bertha Butt and the Butt sisters. I went to campus parties with Darlene and her friends or caught the train to New York City to hang out with Lynn.

I was on a great adventure. The thrill of catching the train into New York City, seeing the bright lights of Times Square and the vast array of shades and shapes of people rushing from place to place was, and is still, a spectacular sight to me. We also enjoyed going to Greenwich Village, where I saw many openly gay men and women, watched break-dancers, magicians, and musicians. I remember listening to Prince's song *Controversy* and thinking the lyrics were so appropriate for the era and the things I was being exposed to for the first time: *Am I black or white? Am I straight or gay? Do I believe in God? I just can't believe all the things people say ... controversy.* This was the era of "the Minneapolis sound." The artist, Prince, was a big influence in my life back then, as he would continue to be. I wanted to act and dress the way he and his band did, and NYC was just the place for that.

When I turned eighteen during my freshman year, I decided to try to find out if my biological mother was looking for me. I had a fantasy about joining a registry upon my eighteenth birthday and being reunited with her. This was the first time I was open about being adopted and being mulatto, but I didn't have the same sense of joy about my birth mother being white because of my new sense of black pride. On a deeper level, however, I didn't care what color she was. I just wanted to find her.

I knew my adoptive mother might be jealous; but I thought she also might be OK with my wanting to find my biological mother, since she herself gave me the information to help me in my search. We were both grateful that my birth mother chose to give me life. I wrote to CUB (Concerned United Birthparents) and ALMA (Adoptee's Liberty Movement Association) in New York for assistance. I filled out registry forms for adoptees to be matched with their biological parents, including all the birth information she would need to find me if she were looking.

As naïve as it may sound, I was confident that it would be a quick match. My mother always told me that my birth mother probably loved me and thought of me often, especially around my birthday. I thought that she would be just as excited as I to finally be able to reunite. It didn't happen as I dreamed. There was no evidence that she was looking for me. This was the beginning of a string of disappointments for me over the next several years. I was once again feeling rejected. What was wrong with me? Why wasn't she looking for me? Why did Greg break my heart? I had so many whys and so many disappointments in such a short period of time. That naïve young girl definitely needed to grow up.

Not only did I need to grow up, my new best friend Michelle also needed to do some growing up. I began to get a peculiar feeling whenever I would hear Michelle talk about her mother's boyfriend. Her mother would often send Michelle places with him while she stayed home. He showed her all of the sights in New York City, almost as if they were dating. He tried to control her, but since he wasn't her father, it didn't seem natural—because it wasn't. After finals, while we were both packing up to go home, she was very defensive about her odd relationship with this man. I told her I suspected he was molesting her. She broke down and told me that he was.

I felt her pain very deeply and knew that I needed to help protect her from this man. I told her that as much as she didn't want to hurt her mother, she had to tell her the truth. She had to tell her the things he was trying to make her do and the mind games he was playing with her. She said her mother was so in love with this man, she may not believe her. How could a mother not believe her own daughter, I thought? She was right. Her mother didn't believe her, or at least she said she didn't. I thought she was in denial.

I never knew how my mother would react to any given situation, but in spite of my fear, I called and asked her if Michelle could come and stay with us. I was shocked when she said, "Both of you—just come home. It will be all right." My mother was so loving and supportive during this time. I had much respect for her coming through the way she did for Michelle. Michelle's mother never believed her and refused to meet me, or my mother, or to come visit Michelle at our home in Massachusetts. Michelle, with no support from her mother, decided to try living with her father in Florida.

I was alone again. Michelle was gone and I didn't know if she would return to college. I was home and had to hear about Greg and that girl again. I also had to get a job to finance the part of my education not covered by my mother's four thousand dollar gift. My mother had a friend named Loretta who worked for the tax department in Connecticut. She not only helped me to get a great job, I rode to work with her every day and she became a mentor to me. This was the summer I fell in love again.

Joey was someone I knew from my early teens. He was another child of mixed heritage—very handsome, with caramel skin and a big curly Afro. I thought he looked like Foster Sylvers—one of my favorite singers when I was in middle school. I had a crush on him but never showed it because of his reputation for being a "player." He even dated a few of my friends. He, like me, had left town and then returned. When he returned, he seemed to be a totally different person. He was wearing a koufe and spent a lot of his time at a mosque in West Springfield. One day, he was walking down State Street and I stopped and gave him a ride home. He talked to me about Islam and let me know that he wanted to get to know me better. I had been so lonely for six months since Greg and I broke up that I wanted someone to love me again. I missed having a boyfriend and was eager to try again.

I'd heard of Islam for the first time in college, but I didn't really know what it was about. I had never attended any religious institution outside of the Christian faith. He told me about his religion and how it changed his life. He took me to meet other Muslims. I quickly fell in love with him—but not with his religion. It just seemed too contradictory to mine. As our love affair progressed that summer, I went from wearing makeup and miniskirts to wearing conservative clothes and no makeup in order to please him. When I called Michelle to tell her, she thought I was crazy or brainwashed. But I believed he really loved me for me—not my clothes or my physical appearance, but the real me inside. By the end of the summer, he traded in his motorcycle to buy a car so that he could drive me back to college. He wanted me to convert to Islam and become his wife. It was wonderful. I felt loved again.

When I returned to college it was difficult for us to maintain our whirlwind romance. We were both students, struggling with our finances. I only saw him when I went home for my birthday or for holidays. We eventually grew apart. I also realized I couldn't become Muslim just to please him. I had to be true to myself. We remained friends and I continued a friendship with his sisters.

I was right back where I started—feeling alone. I couldn't figure out why I was unable to fulfill my dream of getting married and having a "real" family. It sounds pathetic to me now, but that was how I felt at the time. Those were my demons and they would rule a great part of my life. My mother thought that I should have stayed with Greg. She said she thought he and his family loved me and that he took good care of me, except for the cheating. I told her I didn't want to be with a man I couldn't trust. She said, "They all cheat, at least he took good care of you." After a while I started to think she was right. From the time we broke up, Greg kept asking me to take him back. My pride and self-respect wouldn't allow it, however, until my defenses were down. It was only a few months after Joey and I broke up that Greg and I did get back together, and soon became engaged again.

This time I was determined to keep him, so I did everything to try to please him. He liked to drink and go to clubs, so I went along with whatever he enjoyed. I wasn't into drinking but I decided to try drinking beer with him because I had seen my parents drink beer occasionally and they were never drunk. When Greg came to visit on weekends, we would either go to his family's home in Scotch Plains or to a hotel near Club Zanzibar in Newark.

I loved going to that club and feeling like an adult again. I remember one night in particular; a new artist named Madonna was set to perform. There were billboards all around listing her popular songs but they didn't include a photo of her. We arrived early and positioned ourselves in front of the stage. Two black girls and one white girl came onto the stage, dancing. I wondered, "Which one is Madonna?" I was amazed when the blond-haired girl began to sing.

During this time, other people who would later become famous attended Rutgers University. Bill Bellamy, Regina Belle, and Kristin Davis all attended Rutgers while I was there. I remember hearing Regina Belle sing, and hanging out with Bill Bellamy who was friends with my good friend Dana.

They say that when you spend a lot of time with anyone, their ways rub off on you. That was how it was with Greg and me. I began to blend into his world. I managed the beer drinking enough to be sociable and please Greg, but obviously that was not enough for him. He knew that I had always steered clear of drugs and alcohol from the fears of my mother's reaction and other consequences. When I was younger I'd read a book called *Go Ask Alice*, which ingrained in me that using drugs had dire penalties and were not for me. Greg was a weightlifter and took a lot of vitamins. Once he told me to try one of his vitamins. He said it would help me to stay up late so we could hang out.

I took this "vitamin" and began to hallucinate. I don't think I ever was as afraid as I was that night. He said he just wanted us to have fun. When I found out that he had given me mescaline, I was so angry I wanted to kill him. Even after he fell asleep, I was still awake, scared out of my mind. I thought I would hallucinate forever, or never recover or worse yet, have flashbacks for the rest of my life, like I had seen on TV. I was paranoid and claustrophobic. I thank God that I was one of the lucky ones who didn't have lifelong problems because of that one pill. I had always been terrified of any kind of addiction. What I didn't realize was that I was addicted to love. In spite of his cheating and tricking me into taking drugs, I stayed with Greg.

My junior year in college presented a lot of new starts for me. By 1983, I had become well adapted to my college environment. I voted for the first time when the first serious black candidate, Jesse Jackson, ran for president. I survived heartbreaks. I became self-sufficient enough to work and live in New Jersey through the summer months. I was proud of myself for accomplishing all of these milestones. But the best part was that Michelle was coming back to college.

Michelle and I picked right up where we left off, studying and hanging out together while listening to Prince's *Purple Rain* album. Michelle met a nice guy and spent time with him while I was spending time with Greg. I got a car and we traveled to Belmar Beach, Asbury Park, Philadelphia, and New York City. We both had to learn to budget, make our own decisions, and become responsible adults. This was hard for both of us since we both led very sheltered lives before college. Michelle also worked in New Jersey during the summers so that she could avoid going home to where her mother's boyfriend still lived. Her mother wouldn't visit her, but Michelle went to see her when the boyfriend wasn't home. It broke my heart to see her love her mother so much but feel so betrayed by her mother's choice to believe her boyfriend instead of her only child. Her mother eventually married this man and they had a child.

Michelle and I also were very blessed to find two wonderful women who mentored us and became like second mothers to us. One was Freda McLean, a black dean who lovingly guided us both educationally and emotionally. The other was Jackie Bullard who was in charge of Residential Services. She helped me find jobs on campus that not only helped with my finances but also helped me get into the best dorm rooms on campus. I worked as a residential advisor and a programming assistant. Jackie and Freda were our guardian angels.

Having Michelle back on campus was wonderful. Another great thing was my job as a programming assistant, which provided me with my own room and the ability to run various programs on campus. I showed black movies to expose the students to actors and movies many of us had never seen before. During this time, the student body at Rutgers demanded that our university divest from South Africa. Jesse Jackson came to Rutgers and gave a speech encouraging Rutgers to divest. I felt empowered getting involved in making a difference for our people. I wanted to give back. I took another job working with Upward Bound, mentoring local teens, where I met a young girl named Alicia who would become another lifelong friend.

Alicia, Barb, Michelle, and Darlene

During this time, Michelle and I began examining our post-college options. My mother asked me "What will you do with that biology degree if you can't afford to go to medical school?" I'd never thought beyond graduation before. I did my work, was always on the dean's list, and figured I would know what to do by the time I graduated. I began thinking about nursing since my mother, who was 62 years old at the time, was about to graduate from a Licensed Practical Nurse program. I decided to change my major to Nursing even though it would require an additional year of college. Michelle had to do another year because of the year she'd taken off, so I didn't mind. We would do the extra year together.

I loved nursing. I met a lot of nice girls, especially Laura, who in looks and personality reminded me of the TV character Blossom. She was very supportive of me. We were a tight-knit group in this newly formed satellite-nursing program. We had classes and clinical rotations together. We supported one another by car-pooling to our clinical sites and spending a lot of clinical time together. In spite of the supportive and close-knit group, some of my old issues about race reappeared. I was the only black girl in the program and felt like an outsider because of it. Still, I was excited about my new career and decided to become a pediatric nurse.

I enjoyed my chosen field, despite its inherent difficulties. The most heart-wrenching thing I had to deal with was a new kind of discrimination. AIDS was just discovered. Before entering nursing, I thought only gay white men, IV drug abusers, and Haitians contracted AIDS, because that is what was reported in the media. I remember thinking, "I am glad this is a disease I will never have to worry about," because I thought it did not affect heterosexual women.

Not only was I mistaken about that, but also I learned that it affected children. I will never forget the attitude of the staff toward the children afflicted with AIDS. They wanted to throw away the stuffed animals they had played with. The children were isolated and had to eat from disposable Styrofoam trays. There was an immense fear of this new disease, even though we were told it was spread only through contact with blood and bodily fluids. I saw how devastating it was to children when adults were afraid to touch or go near them and my heart went out to them. I thank God that over the years, care of children with AIDS has become much more loving and caring. We have learned to care for their emotional, as well as their physical, needs.

When I finished my fourth year of college, I decided to return to Massachusetts for the summer to plan my wedding. Michelle came home with me and we both got jobs. Michelle started dating a nice guy named Robert in my hometown, and life was great. I was excited about getting married and starting a family. I was also excited to have Michelle with me and to start a career in nursing.

Over the course of the summer, however, I began to get more and more nervous about getting married. I wondered if I could trust Greg. We loved each other but I worried about living the life of my mother with a man I couldn't trust. When it was time to go back to college, Greg went on vacation with his family to North Carolina. I wanted reassurance that everything would be OK. I wanted Greg to call me while he was away with his family, but I didn't hear from him. My mind went crazy despite knowing he was with his family. I began envisioning how terrible it would be to worry like that all the time. Greg's mother once told me that no man could say no to a naked woman if confronted with that option. I could be making a mistake—marrying a man who once cheated on me. "Once a cheater, always a cheater" was another of my mother's sayings. As much as I loved Greg, I never trusted him after he cheated on me. My insecurities took over and I didn't think I could live with an attractive, flirtatious man.

I decided that when he called me, I would tell him how I felt and break off our engagement. I asked Michelle to stay in my room for a few days for moral support so that when he called I would have the courage to tell him. This was the hardest thing I ever had to do. I cried more than I did when he cheated on me. When he cheated, the ball was in his court—he had messed up and I had to break up with him in order to keep my dignity, or so I thought. This time, I was making a decision that would affect the rest of my life and I was afraid I would regret it if it were the wrong one. At the same time, it was a decision I felt I had to make. I called off the wedding.

During the time that I was with Greg, I had remained friends with Pete, the guy from the 'hood I had dated during my junior year in high school, and with Tommy, the first "nice guy" I dated, back in tenth grade. Tommy and I were such good friends that I couldn't see us in a romantic relationship. After breaking off my engagement with Greg, however, Pete and I became more than just friends. I knew my mother wanted me to marry Greg and wouldn't like the idea of my dating Pete again, but I felt I would rather be with an old friend I felt I could trust than to marry a man that I didn't trust. Pete was living in South Carolina since graduating from high school. Over the course of my senior year, thanks to Peoples Airline's cheap flights, Pete and I were able to see each other a couple of times a month. We talked about everything. I shared all of my secrets with him, including my strengths and my weaknesses. He still wanted to be with me despite knowing not only my good qualities but also my not-so-good ones.

time with them in Florida but now it was too late. I wanted my dad to have peace and to be free of pain, but that meant losing him.

The Lord mercifully took him the next day. Family and friends surrounded him. They told me they thought he hung on until he could say goodbye to me. I was so sad. It didn't seem fair to lose my father before he had a chance to see his first grandchild. It was like a nightmare. I couldn't even take time to grieve with my mother. I had to return to work right after the funeral because I had just started a new job.

My mother used to say she hated the holidays. Her brother and mother died near Christmas and that time of year held bad memories for her. I thought my mother was an old Scrooge wanting to ruin my holiday spirit. I had to spend my holidays without other kids—just my older, Scrooge parents. When I was younger, I never understood how she felt. That all changed when my father died just before Christmas. Christmas that year was the hardest holiday for me. I finally had my own home all decorated, and I felt like Scrooge, too. I didn't feel like celebrating. Not only was I grieving my father's death, I also missed my mother, who was having a very difficult time with my father's death.

But I am a survivor, and I survived this period, too. Pete's family was very supportive, as were my new coworkers. The only comfort I felt was the joyful anticipation of my first child's birth. I enjoyed every new stage of my pregnancy. My heart skipped a beat every time the baby kicked or moved. I looked at the ultrasound photos and tried to imagine what she would look like. We went through Lamaze classes and I read every book I could find about pregnancy and parenting. I couldn't wait to breastfeed and to bond with my baby. The nurses at work gave me a baby shower and I prepared the baby's room. I sat in the empty room staring at the Sesame Street images on the wall and the baby clothes in the closet trying to imagine the time when she would finally be there. Most people who aren't adopted don't realize how much it means to have a biological relative; for me this was the most life-changing aspect of the event. During the late stage of my pregnancy, I had a problem keeping up with my nursing job. I was very healthy, but performing duties on a busy pediatric floor will wear out even a non-pregnant woman. I also worried that I wouldn't be able to tell when I was in labor. I asked everyone, "How do you know when it is true labor—not just these Braxton-Hicks contractions?" I was told that I'd just know. I worked right up until the glorious day of her birth.

I woke up in the middle of that May night in 1987 with cramps that kept progressing. They didn't come slowly like I'd been told. After about one hour, they started coming every two to five minutes. At the hospital, my husband and I were escorted to a beautiful, private birthing room. I had planned to do it naturally. Then the pain became unbearable. The epidural became my friend. After it was administered I was able to watch Dr. J's last basketball game on TV without pain. Finally, after a few pushes, out she came. I can't even describe the pure joy I felt when they handed this tiny, 4-pound, 15-ounce, baby girl to me to breastfeed for the first time. It was surreal. My excited husband followed her to the nursery to be examined and cleaned up. I rested. I now felt complete. I did it—I now had a relative that was really a part of me!

Ironically, everyone told me that the baby looked like her father. No one realized how important it had been to me to have her look like me. But it didn't matter. She was mine. Now we had to name her. When we had our marriage ceremony in Massachusetts, there was a little girl at the wedding who had dark eyes, fair skin, and long braided ponytails; she looked just like me when I was young. Her name was Indira, although I thought it was India. We decided we would name our daughter India if she were born with those features. Our daughter's name became India Nicole Peters.

My six weeks at home with her were absolutely joyous. I held her every moment. She slept on my chest and rarely saw her crib. Most parents with a newborn enjoy the time when the baby sleeps; I woke her up to feed her. My mother couldn't come to visit right away but Michelle came immediately and became her godmother. I only wished my father could have seen her. He had been so quiet and distant, I wondered if having a grandchild would have opened him up. I was once told that grandchildren are a parent's greatest joy. My father would never experience that joy, but Pete's parents and extended family enjoyed India. She started out as a scrawny, little, big-eyed baby. She was so small that we worried about her weight right after she was born. We joked that she looked like a hungry little monkey. But by the time she was 2 months old, she was a gorgeous, chunky, little princess. She also started to look more like me!

When my maternity leave was over, I looked forward to going back to work, even though I had to leave my baby. We found a wonderful home day care provider who became like family. Pete was promoted to manager of a new shoe store so we had to move to a little, tiny town called Dalzell, South Carolina, forty-five minutes from Columbia, so he would be near his new job. I didn't want to leave the hospital in Columbia so I commuted four days a week on a special schedule. We found a non-denominational church we loved and where we felt at home. It was very important to me to find a church home where I felt spiritually fed. I missed Pete's sister Marcia who'd lived near us in Columbia, but we had a new support system in Dalzell.

As much as I was enjoying my new life, I was confronted with some prejudices that I had never experienced in the North. Our next-door neighbors, who were outwardly friendly to us, had a Confederate flag in their window facing our home. It was difficult, but I tried to ignore it. This rebel flag was a controversial topic in the 1980s. White southerners viewed it as a part of their history, while black southerners expressed feelings of contempt as it hung from the state capitol. It reminded us of the oppression of the Old south—of slavery and Jim Crow.

One of the things I enjoyed about the South was the food. I thought the food I was raised on was typical Black cuisine, but I learned that it was Southern food and that Southern whites liked it too. On the other hand, I had a hard time dealing with some of the ignorant, racist attitudes. Some of my coworkers asked offensive questions such as, "Do you have to wash black babies' hair?" "Why is their skin so ashy?" "How do you comb their hair?" They had so many "whys" they wanted me to answer. I wanted to ask them ignorant questions about their race in return, but that would just make me just as ignorant as they were. I was constantly asked about my racial background and country of origin. Up North, I was asked if I was Puerto Rican because of the growing Hispanic population in Massachusetts. Down South, Hispanics were not as common. I endured some of the same questions and comments I had hated in my childhood like, "How did you get such 'good' hair?" "Are you mixed with something?" "You don't look like a regular black girl" "You are so educated and well spoken."

I felt as though I had to educate the white people I encountered who held these attitudes. I remember telling a white nurse that if she asked those questions in that tone to another person she was likely to get hurt. In her defense, I don't think she was trying to be hurtful; she was just ignorant. The Southerners I met weren't accustomed to seeing educated blacks. They thought we all were like the images portrayed in the media—an array of negative stereotypes. I also saw less inter-racial dating and marriage in the South. Most of my coworkers with degrees, like RNs, were white. My mother used to say she felt more comfortable in the South because southerners were outwardly racist, whereas northerners would smile at you and then talk about you behind your back. I am not sure which is worse. I know that the comments and racial attitudes in the South became intolerable to me and I wanted to go back home.

Besides the racist attitudes in the South that made me homesick, other problems arose. My husband began to experiment with drugs. This was the last straw. I was having a difficult time adjusting to the South, I missed my friend Michelle, and I was fed up with Pete's irrational behavior, which I learned was caused by his drug use. I was ready to go back to Massachusetts. I called my mother and asked if we could stay with her until we found our own place. She said, "Yes." Pete agreed to make a fresh start by moving back to Massachusetts with India and me and quitting drugs. He found a great job at Monsanto, a local chemical company. I interviewed for a position over the phone and was hired in the pediatric unit at Baystate Medical Center. We looked forward to having a lot more earning potential and I would be back in Massachusetts with my mother and again close to Michelle. I missed them terribly. I couldn't wait to move home. I thought about Prince's song *Sign of the Times: September my cousin tried reefer for the very first time, now he's doing horse; It's June. Sign of the times, mess with your mind. Hurry before it's too late. Let's fall in love, get married, and have a baby.*

The drugs, the marriage, and the baby all were signs of my times and I wanted to hurry home. I missed the familiarity of home. I missed being able to walk down the street and see someone who knew me all of my life. Springfield was part of my history, my past. No matter how nice my coworkers were, they couldn't replace that familiar feeling of home. I couldn't wait to see the places where all of my childhood memories rested and the people with whom I shared the earlier years of my life.

The other reason I couldn't wait to get home was that Michelle began having heart problems. After returning from a trip to Barbados with her boyfriend, she told me she needed a cardiac catheterization in order to figure out why she was feeling so ill. She didn't get the test in a timely manner, probably out of fear. She began to get weaker, but had the fortitude to work and manage her daily activities. Her heart continued to fail until she needed a transplant. That scared me, but she said she wasn't afraid. She was given a 99% chance of survival because she was young and otherwise healthy. She was looking forward to getting a new heart and feeling better. I needed to hurry home to be closer to her.

We packed up our U-haul and prepared to say goodbye to our beautiful country home in Dalzell. My coworkers surprised me with a going away celebration where they presented me with some beautiful handcrafted items that I treasure to this day. My babysitter's family cried when they had to say goodbye to India. We said our farewells and headed back to Massachusetts.

When I returned home, Michelle told me that they had found a heart for her the previous week, on her twenty-fifth birthday. I couldn't be close to her during her surgery and recovery because she was moved to Utah for the procedure. She came through the surgery well and we talked often. She had a lot of support from other transplant patients in the rehabilitation facility. They were provided with mini-apartments until they were stable enough to return home. She sounded happy and healthy, but I was scared. She told me to wait until my birthday to visit her; by then she would be strong enough to enjoy company. That was our plan.

I had to get my life back in order before my trip to Utah, which included starting my new job. Despite the fact that newcomers were seldom able to get day shifts in nursing, I was given a perfect schedule of three twelve-hour day shifts. Mom and I were getting along better than we ever had. She was more relaxed now that I was grown and she didn't have to worry about me. Her work as the strict disciplinarian was over. She said she was happy that I turned out well. Pete and I found a new home with a garage and deck on a little cul-de-sac. I couldn't wait to move in and get settled. I was back home with my old friends and family life was great. But once again, trouble was right around the corner.

I was watching television in the den with Pete and India, who was now 16 months old. The telephone rang and my mother told me it was Michelle's boyfriend.

"Hi, Renny. How are you? Is Michelle there with you?" I asked excited at the thought of talking to my friend.

"No, Barb. She's not here," he said in a strange tone of voice.

My heart began to race and I felt a sense of panic come over my body. I didn't know what to say.

"She's not here. That is why I am calling."

"Where is she?" I asked.

"Michelle went into ICU a week ago—

Before he could finish I said, "Oh my God, can I come out and visit her?"

"No, Barb. She was in ICU for a week. She began to reject her transplanted heart and fell into a coma."

"I still want to see her, even if she is in a coma," I said. "What hospital is she in?"

"Please Barb, let me finish. Her family didn't want anyone to know she was in the ICU, which is why I didn't call you sooner. I am calling you tonight because Michelle never came out of her coma. I'm sorry. She died today."

I couldn't speak.

"Barb? Are you there?" he asked.

All I could do was cry.

"Barb?"

"I'm here. I wish I could have seen her to let her know how much I loved her," I said.

"She knew. We all knew. She loved you just the same."

I felt my whole world come crashing down on me. I thought I was having a bad dream. I will never forget the initial pain. It felt as if a big piece of me died at that instant. I wanted to just wake up from that dream and have everything be OK. I cried and cried inconsolably. My mother and Pete kept asking me what was wrong and I couldn't even speak. I finally was able to tell them that my best friend Michelle was gone.

I couldn't understand why no one had told me about Michelle's worsening condition. Then it dawned on me that Michelle's mother probably blamed me for their estrangement. This may have been her ultimate revenge. I would have flown to Utah in a heartbeat if I knew she was not doing well. I planned to visit her in just one month. We were going to be living near each other again. She was my best friend and confidante. I was closer to her than anyone else. I hadn't had a chance to say goodbye and I couldn't imagine my life without her. It was only a month since her surgery and she assured me that she would be stronger by the time we planned our visit. Her boyfriend told me that she was unconscious the entire time she was in ICU and that she wouldn't have known I was there anyway. That didn't matter to me. I would have been able to hold her hand and tell her how much she meant to me. Her mother took that away from me. Michelle's boyfriend gave me the details for her final arrangements so that I could at least see her one more time.

Pete, India, and I drove to New York City for Michelle's funeral services in Queens. It was the first time I saw her mother, her mother's husband—the man who'd hurt my friend—and their child. Dean McLean and Michelle's boyfriend were the only people I knew at the funeral.

An older woman who resembled Michelle walked up to me and asked me to follow her to a small room where some of the family had gathered.

"Hi, Barb. I am Franco's mom, Michelle's grandmother. Come give me a hug."

"Michelle told me a lot about you," I said as I embraced her.

"Michelle also told us so much about you. You were the best friend she ever had and you were always there to support each other."

"Is that her goddaughter India?" another woman asked.

"Yes, this is India." I said.

"I recognize her from her photos. Everyone, this is Michelle's goddaughter India and her friend Barbara," Michelle's grandmother said.

Many family members came over to hug me and introduce themselves. Some of them I recognized from the many family photos I had seen; others I did not, but they all seemed to know about me. They wanted to meet India and me and tell us how important we were to my friend. They wanted to thank me for helping her, especially during the time she left home. I told them how much I loved her and how much I'd miss her. Then Michelle's grandmother handed me a box.

"This is the bracelet you sent to Michelle for her birthday. We had to take it off before her surgery. I was holding onto it for her but now I want you to have it," she said.

I started to cry again as I remembered the day I chose the bracelet and how I mailed it to her early so that I would be sure it arrived before her birthday. Her grandmother and I then walked out of the room together.

Everyone but Michelle's mother and stepfather comforted and supported me. They never acknowledged my presence. I wanted to grab that man and choke him. How dare he act like the caring stepfather after what he did to her? I wanted to shout out loud and tell everyone what a monster he was. Fortunately, Dean McLean kept me in control. She said to let it go. God would take care of it.

I walked up to the casket to say goodbye. I felt her hair. It was the only thing on her that still felt alive. I didn't want to leave her side. I wanted to crawl into the casket with her, but other people needed to say goodbye, so I had to move on. I spotted some flowers with ribbons saying "From Your Loving Mother." I felt sick and wanted to die. What a façade, I thought. Then I realized that no matter what had happened in the past, Michelle was still her daughter and she loved her. It must have hurt her deeply to know that she turned her back on her daughter when she needed her most and now she was gone. As much as I disrespected her, I also pitied her for her loss and for having to live with what she did for the rest of her life. At least the secret scandal was buried with Michelle.

Watching Michelle being lowered into the ground was unbearable. Her boyfriend had put a picture of the two of them in the casket with her and my heart was breaking for him, too. He loved her as much as I did. I didn't think I would ever have a friend like Michelle and I didn't know how I would live without her.

The pain of grief never goes away, but at least the intensity lessens. As I went through this process, I felt guilty because I realized that I cried more and mourned longer after Michelle died than I did when my dad died. She was my best friend, my sister, and my confidante. She knew me better than anyone else, even my husband. It was during this time that I also realized I didn't know my husband as well as I thought.

I'd begun to recognize how very jealous and controlling Pete was. He felt threatened when I lost weight and got my figure back after having India. He began talking about having another child right away. I always wanted a big family, but I enjoyed having plenty of time to devote to India. I looked forward every day to the time we spent together. I didn't think I could love another child as much. Maybe that is the way some parents feel about their first-born. In reality, there is enough love for all of their children.

After another sad holiday season I discovered I was pregnant again. It was the spark of happiness that helped me out of my depression. I was once again looking forward to having another blood relative. Because India was so small, I had frequent ultrasounds. At about six months into my pregnancy, right before the Fourth of July, the doctor told us that this little baby girl wasn't growing properly. After much contemplation and discussion, Pete, my doctor, and I decided it would be best if I stopped working and stayed home for the rest of my pregnancy. I was happy to be able to spend the next six months at home with India, taking care of myself. I was looking forward to giving birth to another healthy baby girl and staying home for the entire holiday season. It would be a way to replace the sadness of the previous holiday seasons with happier memories.

For the next six months I spent every waking hour with India. We took daily walks to the park and played games together. I read her stories and worked on potty training. I couldn't wait to see my new baby. My love for this unborn child grew the way it had for India. Everyone was right; I did have enough love to go around. I was thrilled about giving India a baby sister, something I'd always wanted. India went to sibling classes to get ready for the new baby. Everyone was excited.

One night, I fell asleep watching a documentary about cultural pain rituals. I awoke to pains in my stomach and I thought I was dreaming. It wasn't a dream; I was in labor again. Twelve hours later, on that September morning in 1989, Brittany Michelle Peters was born. She weighed 6 pounds, 15 ounces, and was a beautiful baby with thick, curly hair. I felt even more complete. My college friend Dana came to visit, and I felt like I was in heaven. Pete and I lived near both of our families. My mom and I were now close. My children would have siblings, grandparents, and aunts, all the things I didn't have.

I was able to stay home from work with my beautiful daughters for four months and celebrate Christmas. We played Santa Claus for India and she was happy. She loved her baby sister and wanted to help me take care of her. She called her Britt-Britt, a nickname that stuck. I had everything I wanted except that Michelle couldn't see her. At least she would carry Michelle's name. Michelle would never be forgotten. Life was great again; that is, until the next storm.

The next crisis came when I discovered that our checking account had insufficient funds. There were a lot of withdrawals and checks were being returned. Since this never happened before, I thought it must be a mistake. I was very organized and always maintained our finances without any problems. I went to the bank and found out it wasn't a mistake. Pete had been withdrawing money for drugs. He confessed that he was using cocaine. I told him if he didn't get help I would leave him. He went to an outpatient drug program and went into recovery. He gave up not only cocaine but alcohol as well. He learned about addictions and how to stay clear of anything or anyone that would tempt him.

Pete worked a lot of overtime and I went back to work. We saved up enough money for a down payment on a house. We found a beautiful, four-bedroom home with a large living room with a fireplace, and a formal dining room like at my mother's house. It had a den like my old home and a nice backyard with a swing set. It was only the second home we looked at and I immediately fell in love with it. It was only two miles from my mother's home in Sixteen Acres. She offered to help with our down payment to reduce our mortgage payments. On April 12, 1990, we closed on our first home. I felt I had accomplished everything I wanted. I had a great job, beautiful daughters, my husband had gone through recovery and had a great job, and my mother and I were close. We had the American dream. But still something was missing. I needed the Lord in my life.

During our search for a church home, we attended a church with Pete's family. It was nice, but not like the church in South Carolina. We visited many churches but they didn't give us what we needed. It was many years later that I found a place where I was truly spiritually fed.

Life was good for a while. Pete was a very doting, involved father. He was involved in every aspect of the girls' lives. He fed them, bathed them, and was very proud of his smart, sweet, lovable daughters. India went to preschool. Pete and I worked opposite schedules so that one of us was always home with Brittany. Our lives centered on the girls. The only time we spent away from them was when we went to the Bahamas for our fifth anniversary. Even during our trip, we constantly talked about the girls and missed them. Every holiday centered on them and our aim was to keep them happy and feeling loved.

Some of the most celebrated holidays in our house were the girls' birthdays. I've always thought that birthdays are each person's very special day. On Brittany's third birthday, I hired a clown for her party. Pete surprised us all by also hiring a pony for the day. We awoke to hearing neighing in the backyard. The neighborhood children had a wonderful time getting pony rides and playing at our home. More important, Brittany felt very special that day. India was daddy's girl and Brittany was mommy's girl, but soon I would be all that both girls had.

India and Brittany

5

Codependency, Divorce, and Dating

Not until we are lost, do we begin to understand ourselves.

—*Henry David Thoreau*

Over the next few months, Pete's behavior changed again. He became extremely jealous, argumentative, possessive, and controlling. He told me what clothes he wanted me to wear and called me the minute I left work to be sure I was on my way home. Greg's house was near the hospital and he wanted to make sure I had no time to go near my ex-fiancé. I constantly tried to reassure him that he could trust me, but it didn't matter. He objected to my talking to any men, even coworkers or casual acquaintances.

On one occasion, Pete and I were out shopping. He parked the car in front of a store and said he would be right back. One of my ex-boyfriends walked past our car and waved hello. I waved back. Pete came out of the store and was very angry. He didn't speak to me the entire drive home. At first, I didn't understand why he was so upset. I knew it couldn't be just because I waved at someone. When we got home, he said, "Why did you wave at Lewis?"

"Because he waved hello to me!" I said.

"What would have happened if I didn't come back to the car?" he said.

"Nothing. It was just a wave," I said, thinking how silly this conversation was.

"I bet you still like him don't you?" he said."

"No. I dated him a long time ago. You need to stop trippin'!" I said, feeling very frustrated.

"Who are you talking to like that?" he said in a louder voice.

"YOU. And this is crazy!" I returned, growing tired of the conversation.

"You need to learn to respect me!" he yelled.

"I don't want you talking to him or any other guys while you are my wife!" he demanded.

"That is so stupid!" I said as I began to walk away. Before I knew what was happening, he grabbed me.

"Get your hands off of me!" I screamed.

"You better not ever disrespect me like that again," he yelled as he raised his hand to hit me. He pulled my hair and dragged me down the stairs into the living room. I fought back and then called the police. They came quickly and removed him from our house. He said he was sorry and he would never do it again but I knew he still had to leave.

My mother had told me, "Never let a man lay his hands on you!" At first I blamed myself, thinking I had provoked him. I later realized that I hadn't provoked him, and even if I had, he should have never touched me. When he returned a few days later, I told him that if it ever happened again he would be gone forever.

After the holiday season of 1992, things got worse. He began to threaten me again. He didn't want me to go anywhere alone. I always had to take the girls with me. I felt like a caged bird. He tried to convince me to have another child. I think he thought I would be unattractive and easier to control if I were pregnant. I realized at this point that he was using drugs again.

I saw the devastating effects drug abuse had on his sister. I knew I could never live under those conditions nor did I want my girls exposed to those influences. When I began to talk about separating from my husband, no one could understand it. From all outward appearances, Pete was a hard-working, generous husband and a good father. He showered me with attention and gifts. He called me at work to tell me that he loved me, sent me roses, and came to visit me with our girls during my breaks at work. He was very sweet and loving but he also could be very controlling and argumentative. We all have our good side and bad side, and no one knew what was going on behind closed doors. I knew, however, what was best for the girls and me. I never wanted them exposed to drugs or violence in our home. My job was to love and protect them at all costs. I knew it was time to end our marriage. I told Pete I wanted a separation. I felt in my heart that I no longer wanted to be married to him but didn't talk divorce at first for fear he wouldn't leave. I told him I just needed some time to think about things.

When we separated, I felt relieved. I finally felt at peace. He wanted to go into marriage counseling, but I didn't think it would work. I was really fed up. I finally told my friends about the drug use and the violence I had endured. They were all amazed because they had only seen the façade. My girlfriends, my mother and Joey, with whom I'd reconnected, gave me moral support and guidance through that difficult time.

Although she gave me moral support, my mother thought that I should have stayed in the marriage for the sake of my children. She also knew that I was an adult and had to make my own decisions. I knew that whether or not we saw eye to eye, she was my mom and would support my decision. She was afraid I would lose my house. I was afraid too, but I was more afraid of living with someone who was jealous, violent, and abusing drugs. Eventually, I told her everything and she understood.

Once when I was out with a few of my girlfriends, Pete ran into us and told me if he ever saw me out again, he would hurt me. There was a part of me that was afraid but there was another part of me that had my mom's strength. Because I thought it was best for our daughters to have a good relationship with their father, I continued to let him visit the girls whenever he wanted. He was always kind and gentle in front of them, until one day he pushed me into the girls' playroom. I told them to go upstairs. He said, "If I can't have you, nobody can have you," and began to threaten me even more. I really thought he meant it this time. I convinced him to leave quietly by telling him that he was upsetting the girls. The next day I obtained a restraining order. I had had enough. After that, he threatened to stop giving me child support unless I stopped going out and stayed in the house. He was always a faithful provider and I didn't believe he would withhold financial support. I thought he was just angry. I was wrong.

Pete carried out his threat and stopped providing child support, even though he knew that I was working only part-time. My mother taught me to "Never have children that you cannot afford to care for alone and never get bills you cannot pay for yourself." But I now found myself with two small children, a large mortgage, credit card bills, and household expenses, and no savings. We had depleted our savings when we bought our new home. Any chance of reconciling with Pete was over. I could never live with a man who would abandon his family like that. I got my full-time job back and worked overtime as much as I could. Pete's mom and my mom helped out with babysitting while I worked the long hours needed to support the three of us.

What Pete did next was even worse. He stopped visiting the kids. I recalled something that Pete's mother once told me. She said that most men only show love to kids while they are living with them. When Pete was a senior in high school, he had a son who he never financially supported and rarely saw. It made no sense for a man to go from being an involved, doting father who visited his children every day and provided financial support, to not seeing or taking care of them. He never even called them. It may have been the drugs. It may have been to punish me because I wouldn't take him back. Maybe his mother was right. He didn't live with them any more; and maybe he didn't want to be bothered with them anymore. The reason didn't matter. The fact remained that his behavior was unfair to the girls. My mother helped me get a lawyer and I filed for divorce.

Filing for divorce saddened me not only for losing my dream of a perfect family but also for the loss of Pete's family who had become such a large part of my life. My relationship with them became strained when we separated. When I finally told them about the threats and abuse, they didn't believe me until one day he came to my house and I called his mother. He needed money and he ripped a gold necklace off my neck in front of the kids. His mother finally glimpsed the reality of our circumstances.

As much as I hated him at the time, I knew Pete needed help. He had been such a good person. I wanted that good person back, at least for his children. India and Brittany were heartbroken by their father's neglect.

I contacted a friend of Pete's and we planned an intervention with his daughters and his parents. We tried to convince him to get help for his drug problem before he lost his job and his life. We thought if he saw the girls he would agree. I agreed to a plan to let him spend the night with his girls and then check him into a program the next day. He agreed but on the way home, he opened the door to my van and jumped out. I called his mother and told her that if they wanted to try to help him, it would have to be without me. I was not willing to traumatize the girls any longer. Shortly afterwards, he lost his job. Health insurance from his job was the only thing we had received from him for months as it was in place before we separated, and with the loss of his job, that was gone. When I received this news I was at work and I became so upset I had to go home. I realized at that point that I, myself, needed help. I sought out a therapist to help me with my stress and anxiety.

With the help of my counselor, I learned that I was a classic, textbook martyr/rescuer/enabler and a co-dependent person. I read a book my therapist recommended to me called *Codependent No More*, by Melody Beattie. The text described me precisely. I seemed to be drawn to people that needed help. I'd even chosen a helping profession. Helping others made me feel worthwhile. I didn't realize that trying to fix other people's problems was not healthy for me. The book gave practical tools on how to stop trying to work on other people's problems and start taking care of myself. That is what I began to do. Before I began counseling, I didn't understand why I put up with some things I put up with or why I felt so lost and unable to care for myself. Instead, I spent time trying to take care of the needs of others. I took the tools that I learned and began to focus on what was most important in my life.

Taking care of my children and me became my primary focus. Everything and everyone else was secondary. I learned that I shared no blame for Pete's drug abuse and its consequences. He had to own his illness and control his own life. If he didn't care for his kids, I would do it alone. And do it I did.

I didn't let the girls know that their father was not supporting us, but money was scarce. I was working all the time, but barely making ends meet. I tried to overcompensate for Pete's absence by giving my girls whatever they wanted. I let them take dance lessons until I absolutely couldn't afford it. I tried to make their birthdays and holidays special. One Christmas, the girls wanted a Nintendo. Pete agreed to buy it for them and I agreed to buy the games. The girls were very excited. Then, a couple of days before Christmas, his girlfriend called me to tell me that he spent all of his money and had no plans to honor the promise he made to the girls. I decided to buy the Nintendo myself and say it was from him.

Through therapy I realized that I had been enabling him to be an absent, unreliable father by covering up and making excuses for his behavior. I learned to stop enabling even though it meant that the girls would eventually find out they weren't a priority in his life.

As time went on, Pete stopped harassing me and I finally gained some peace. He didn't support us financially, but at least he left me alone. I became lonely and started to date again. My longtime friend Joey said he still loved me but his religion forbade him to be with a woman who was still legally married. I understood, and we decided to remain platonic friends.

I started dating a nice guy named Dexter. We'd attended the same high school but I hadn't known him because he graduated a year behind me. Because he was the first guy I dated since filing for divorce, he had to deal with Pete and Pete's friends. He didn't mind. He had a daughter the same age as Brittany and we got along well. We even had a mutual friend, my foster-sister Angela. One of his friends was dating her. I hadn't seen her in a long time and I enjoyed hanging out with Dexter and with her. I visited his father's church with him and went to his mother's home for the holidays. We took our kids to the amusement park, visited the Mohawk trail with my friends, and shared other social events and gatherings with our friends as well as quiet time in our homes. It was the first time I had been happy in quite a while. I wasn't looking for love, just companionship, and he seemed to fit the bill. I was enjoying all of the time we spent together until I found out he was secretly seeing another woman—a white woman. He denied it of course, but I knew it was true. I felt like I was living my mother's life. I remembered my mom asking my father, "Am I not light enough for you?" That is how I felt—not light enough. My old racial issues began to resurface. We parted as friends.

I may not have been lucky in love but I was truly blessed with my friendships. When my girls went to visit their father's family, I was lonely, but I had great friends, and their families, who always made me feel loved and welcome in their homes. My mother had since remarried and she often spent time with her new husband and his family, so I was especially grateful for my friendships during this time.

One of my friends, Dawn, is very much like me. She is biracial, with thick, curly hair. She is open and talkative and we have similar interests. Our friendship began when I was dating Greg. We kept in touch and rekindled our friendship when I returned to Springfield. She was one of my friends who thought Pete and I had the perfect home and family. She used to tell me that she looked up to me, as I seemed to have a charmed life—with a great husband and kids and a nice, newly purchased home when I was only 26 years old. We grew even closer as the façade of a charmed life faded. I asked her to be my girls' godmother and she happily agreed. We began spending more time together. We liked to go out dancing and to just hang out. I became friendly with her brother Doug whom I was very close to when I was engaged to Greg, as well as her sister Monife. Monife and Dawn had different personalities but got along very well. I envied that because I'd always wished I had a sister. I had only had friends that were like sisters to me, like Lynn, and my "almost-sister," Angela. Dawn said we were so close that she felt like a sister to me and that is how she began to refer to me, as her sister, just like Lynn had.

Monife, Dawn, and Barb

Dawn's parents were very warm and inviting, and we grew close. They had been married during the turbulence of the 1960s, and although they were from different races and religions, had survived the test of time. They were very involved in their children's lives. The girls were involved in dance and pageants. Dawn was once crowned queen of a local African American festival. Mrs. Marshall was white and she made sure her daughters had pride in all aspects of their cultures. She taught them about her Jewish faith. They also learned about Christianity and Islam. They were proud of all aspects of their heritage and were encouraged to live their lives as individuals—not according to one race, one color, or one religion.

In the 1960s, it was customary for the white member of a mixed marriage to assimilate into the black culture because society saw the children as African-American. Often, the black community accepted these mixed-race children more readily than did the white community. Dawn's parents were involved in the black community and with their extended family members. I viewed them as the most well rounded family I knew, and we became a part of that family. My girls and I were always expected to be at their home during the holidays.

I have another friend, Veronica, who is very different from me. I am outgoing and talkative. She is quiet and reserved. My idea of a good time was hanging out with a group of people or going out to a club. Hers was more intimate and quiet. She didn't like crowds or noise. We both worked as nurses on the same pediatric unit. At first, because she didn't share much about herself, I thought she didn't trust me and didn't want to be my friend. That was not the case. She was just more of an observer than a talker, whereas I was more of a talker than an observer. I have learned more from Veronica than any of my other friends, because of our differences. She has helped me to see the world from a different perspective. We complement and continue to bring out the best in each other.

Veronica's family was another example of the kind of family I had always dreamed of having. She had two older sisters, Jackie and Deirdre, who looked out for her. She was the apple of her father's eye and her mom's pride and joy. She had aunts and uncles and a grandmother who were involved in her daily life. They enjoyed each other's company. They were successful and helped whoever was in need. When it came time for one of the family members to go to college, it was a family affair to provide whatever was needed throughout the college career. I thought Veronica had a charmed life. She went to private school. She didn't get spanked, and had a great social life. She was beautiful and smart. There were times that I wished I could be in her shoes, but she helped me realize that I should be thankful for my own life and its blessings.

Jackie, Veronica, and Barb in Jamaica

Since I always wanted siblings, anyone with a brother or sister seemed fortunate. Veronica's family was warm and receptive to my children and me. We always had a place to go and a hot meal waiting. Just like the Marshall family, they included us in their family celebrations. In spite of all the love and warmth from both of these families, I still felt like I didn't belong. It took me another ten years to realize that those feelings were due to my own insecurities and lack of self-identity. I was considered part of their families despite not being born to their families. I had many unfounded insecurities regarding relationships, but always felt confident and secure when it came to my education and career.

During this time, I began to make major accomplishments in my nursing career. I was encouraged to climb our clinical ladder for advancement and specialize in clinical education. It didn't take long for me to rise to the top, level four, and become the pediatric unit educator. I got a nice pay raise and felt like I was a success at something again. I was able to work weekdays and be home with my girls for holidays and weekends. I developed a clinical preceptor program on our unit and trained all of the new nurses. I also chaired our unit's recruitment and retention committee. Other nurses who were making the same kinds of gains were going back to school for their Master's degrees. I thought about it, but decided that my children needed me more than I needed another degree at the time.

With all the perks that went along with my new position, some of the same old racial issues that I had dealt with at the hospital in South Carolina began to arise. Before becoming a clinical educator, I belonged to a very diverse group. There were white, black, and Hispanic, female and male nurses on our pediatric unit. We even had a black manager named Janet who was my friend. I enjoyed my coworkers and we all got along well. I soon found out that it was not like that throughout the hospital. At the educator meetings, I was the only black woman and I felt isolated again.

In an attempt to raise some awareness among the predominantly white staff, I proposed educational programs that dealt with cultural diversity and sensitivity. At first they were denied, but then accepted on a trial basis. I contracted with an esteemed local trainer on the topic, Dale Parker, who taught a workshop on cultural diversity that I thought was wonderful. My white coworkers didn't agree. Dale explained societal prejudice and racism. They didn't seem to believe that the problem existed. A problem cannot be dealt with unless it is recognized as a problem. That goes for codependency, addiction, and social ills like racism and prejudice. It seems as though people for whom oppression is not a reality of daily life want to pretend that these social injustices don't exist. They are simply in denial.

The staff decided to remain in denial, which frustrated me. Once we were trying to choose a place to meet outside of work. Like most people of color, I am very good at what is called "switching." We have to learn how to live in two cultures—our own, and the majority culture. I have learned to meet people where they are on an individual basis. That doesn't always mean that I like where they are. I went to holiday gatherings with DJ's playing music I didn't enjoy and eating food I didn't especially like. In an environment with only a few people of color, there is an assumption that we enjoy the same food, music, and social events. When I asked about doing something totally different, they looked at me like I was from another planet. It had never occurred to any of them that there were other types of music, or different restaurants, or even other neighborhoods than the ones they were accustomed to.

I tried to give them a philosophical example of how it feels to be in the minority. I asked how they would feel if every social gathering were held in a predominantly black neighborhood. I remember once describing the Hill-McKnight area with its great mansions, clubs, and soul food restaurants that I frequented. I told them about the world that I love—my culture, my black people. I asked them how they would feel being the one white person in a group and having to "switch" to another culture. It never dawned on any of them what life was like for me.

During this time, I saw a television special on *20/20* about race in America. They showed a hidden camera video of the day in the life of a black man and a day in the life of a white man. They chose men of similar age, education, and appearance except for color. Both men went through different scenarios such as looking for an apartment, shopping in a clothing store and hailing a cab. It showed how preferential treatment was always given to the white man while the black man was ignored and denied access. My coworkers thought that these were isolated incidents. I can't imagine how hard it was during the time when my mother was young, when racism was even more blatant. The older I got, the more respect and love I felt for my mother for the struggles she suffered while still remaining strong. She taught me what I needed to do in order to get ahead.

In March of 1994, our unit was preparing for a pediatric conference in New Orleans. I was given the honor of sharing a presentation on my work with the recruitment and retention committee at the conference. I couldn't afford a vacation during this time and was excited about being given an all-expense paid trip to an exciting place like New Orleans. I recalled all of the wonderful things my mother told me about New Orleans. I looked forward to my first trip there and doing my poster presentation. I called my former coworkers in South Carolina and found out that two of them would be attending. I was very excited. I called Jose, a high school friend of mine who lived in Florida, and told him about my upcoming trip. He decided to drive from Tampa to New Orleans to hang out with me. I thought that was very thoughtful, especially since we were only friends.

It was a great trip. Between working and caring for my girls on my own, I rarely had "me time." Even going to the gym had to be worked into my schedule and required finding a babysitter. I was happy to not have to worry about cooking or cleaning up after anyone, and enjoyed being able to go to the hotel health club, as well as taking some quiet time alone before the conference started.

New Orleans was an exciting place. They had street magicians, parades, parties, and entertainment on every street. My coworkers and I went to Pat O'Brien's and got on stage to perform karaoke to the song *Wild Thing*. It was refreshing to enjoy my coworkers in a place other than work or in our hometown.

Jose gave me a real treat and took me to the zoo because he knew I loved animals. I was also impressed that he would drive so far to hang out with me and was a perfect gentleman expecting nothing in return.

Being able to see my old friends from South Carolina, socialize with my coworkers, attend an informational conference, and have a great guy show me the town was all more than I had expected. The only bad part was that I missed my girls. My roommate during the trip thought Jose was a great guy and that I should consider dating him. Having been in two long-distance relationships in the past, I didn't think it was a good idea. We hung out as friends, but as time went on, he changed my mind.

After the conference, Jose kept calling. He visited Springfield regularly and requested that his private investigative firm give him work in Massachusetts. I decided to give him a chance, even though I was still waiting for my divorce to be final. He didn't seem to mind; he said he just wanted to be with me.

Jose was the first man I dated who was not black. He was Puerto Rican. Most of his friends from high school were black and he dated a lot of black girls. I thought at first he was of mixed heritage like me. I remember our first real date when he arrived in Massachusetts. He asked me where I wanted to go and I jokingly said, "Six Flags in New Jersey." I missed going there after graduating from college. He said, "OK. Let's do it!" And we did. I also attended a wedding with him during this time, and met a lot of his friends and family. This is where I began to feel the culture shock.

I didn't think my being black was a big deal. I saw all people of color as the same. I learned that not everyone saw things from my perspective. I didn't realize that people of color discriminated against other people of color or other ethnicities. I learned how naïve I was, once again, when it came to racial issues. When I was around some of Jose's friends, I got some of the same questions and comments about my looking black and not having black hair. I also heard, "Are you sure you're not part Spanish, you look Spanish" or "You don't look like a black girl." The same angry feelings I felt when I lived in South Carolina revisited me. Again, I told them that African Americans are just like Hispanics—they come in all shades, all hair types, and all income levels. I felt uncomfortable again.

His parents were very receptive to me despite my not being Hispanic. One of his relatives recounted a story about how when he first came to the United States, he, despite being dark in complexion, was considered white, while his black partner was seen as black. We both thought it was strange, yet that is how things were in those days. I began to hear derogatory comments about black people when someone didn't know I was listening or when others just assumed I was Hispanic.

I also heard prejudicial comments about other Hispanic groups. I learned that some Puerto Ricans say negative things about Mexicans and Cubans. I thought that was bizarre. They all spoke the same language. I thought they were kindred spirits. I was wrong again. I felt like a fly on the wall. I found out that people of all races and colors are prejudiced against other people who have even the slightest differences. I'd thought my mother was cynical when she talked about how the world really was. I was finding out that she knew these things because she had experienced them, just as I was now.

Despite what I experienced with some of his acquaintances, I didn't feel the cultural difference with Jose. In fact, my new boyfriend and I had a lot in common. We enjoyed amusement parks, games, the same type of music, going to clubs, and traveling. He also had two daughters and they got along well with my girls. Jose gave my daughters nicknames. He called India "Indiana Jones" or "my Indian" and he called Brittany "Thunderstorm" because she was so active and energetic. The girls liked Jose. At this time in my life, I was content living with just the girls. I wasn't looking for another husband, so I didn't mind that Jose lived in Florida. He visited us and showered me with love and attention and made my girls feel special. I only wanted honesty and respect for us long as we were together. I was finally free of the need for a picture-perfect family. I was content with my girls, my friends, and my mom.

In the fall of 1994, my mother invited Veronica and me to take our children on a vacation to Florida during one of the weeks she had her time-share in Orlando. Veronica was in the process of adopting a little girl we had both grown to love while she was a patient on our pediatric unit. Jose went back to Florida while we were on vacation to show us around the state. We went to many places including Busch Gardens, Wet and Wild, and Disney World.

We had a wonderful time except that while we were at Jose's Florida home, I sensed that he was still in contact with his former girlfriend. Feelings of distrust began to creep into our relationship, and by the time 1995 rolled around, we had stopped seeing each other. He continued to call me whenever he was in town, but I knew we could only be friends. You can't have a relationship without trust. One Valentine's Day weekend, I heard that Jose was coming to town and was planning to surprise me. I decided to avoid him by spending the night at a friend's house. By this time, my divorce was final and I didn't want any ties to bind me. As I was on my way home the next day, a car pulled up behind me.

It was déjà vu. My old boyfriend Joey beeped the horn and asked me to pull over on State Street, just as he'd done thirteen years earlier. He said that he had heard my divorce was final and wanted to know if we could get together. I said yes. For the first time in my life, I wasn't looking for a man to make me feel complete. I enjoyed my life. My girls and my mom were all the family I needed. I'd once heard that when you stop looking for something, that is when you find it. That is what happened to me.

6

New Beginnings

o o o o o o o o o o o o o o o o o o o o o o o o o o o o o o o
Think of the beauty still around you and be happy.

—*Anne Frank*

Joey and I met the next day and went bowling with my girls. It was 1995. India and Brit were now seven and five years old, respectively. When they asked me who he was, I told them he was an old friend. Joey and I fell in love back when I was just eighteen, and he was a very supportive friend when I first separated from Pete. Now, here he was in my life again.

Joey had recently broken up with his girlfriend and she was expecting a baby in a few months. He said that she was very volatile and jealous. I could identify with his situation having been married for seven years to a similarly jealous husband. I wanted to be supportive even if we were going to be just friends. I was happy to see his parents again and it brought back a lot of good memories. It didn't take long for things to change.

Joey told me that he'd always loved me and wanted to marry me ever since we were teenagers. He hesitated to get into a relationship with me when I was first separated but now I was divorced. I thought it was ironic that I was hearing these things when I had finally resigned myself to being alone and was quite comfortable with it. We began seeing each other daily during the spring of 1995, and after only one month, he started talking about getting married. I thought at first that he was just joking. He never stayed in a relationship with any woman for very long. As time went on, I realized just how serious he was. He wanted to get married on July third because he said he wanted every anniversary to be a big celebration like the Fourth of July. I didn't tell anyone at first because it all seemed so sudden. It felt surreal and I was waiting for some storm to rain on my parade, as it usually did.

One of the things I admired about Joey was that he wanted to be an active part of his new daughter, Porsche's, life. Her mother gave him a difficult time about seeing her, since they weren't together. He endured their conflicts for the sake of his daughter. I think one of the reasons I wanted to marry him was because he was a dedicated father despite the fact that he and his child's mother were not on good terms. This was very different from the man I had been married to, who was a devoted dad as long as we were together and an irresponsible father when we weren't. Joey also wanted to be involved with my girls.

My mother gave me her blessing. She thought Joey truly loved me and was a good person. He was willing to take on the role of husband and stepfather. We decided on a small, private ceremony. We went to New York City to buy our rings and to Vermont for the marriage license. Veronica gave me a bridal shower even though she was pregnant and very close to her delivery date. Dawn agreed to be my maid of honor and Alicia was coming from New Jersey to be at my side. All was calm again, until the storm of Porsche's mother came into our lives.

Porsche's mother knew that Joey was in a relationship with someone who was a nurse but didn't know who it was. After Porsche was born, she made a point to find out whom I was. She made some inquiries about me with her visiting nurse and at my job, and one of the nurses became concerned about her inquiries and reported it. Porsche was about to be admitted for some medical testing at the pediatric unit where I worked. I requested to be on another unit while she was there, to decrease the chances of any conflict with her mother. Before Porsche was admitted, I decided to call her mother to let her know that I respected her as Porsche's mother, that I meant her no ill will, and that I would not be around when her daughter was in the hospital. That was not the good idea I'd thought it was. She called me obscene names and told me that she was the most beautiful girl Joey had ever been with and she knew that an ugly black girl could never compare with her.

I realized my attempts to make peace were futile. Maybe I should have known she had some issues about race. Joey, who also had a mixed-race heritage of black, white, and Native American, told me she was worried about having a dark-skinned baby or one with bad hair. He said she'd even used the "N word" in his presence. She continued with threatening, obscene remarks and my old feelings of anger about race arose. She was a very light-skinned Puerto Rican girl with bleached-blond hair, and I thought, "How dare she judge me just because I'm black." She didn't know me and had never seen me. I decided to give her space and stay out of her way. I was going to be married in a few weeks and we didn't need the drama.

Since she couldn't get to me, Porsche's mother decided to punish Joey by not allowing him to see Porsche. He made arrangements to take her to court to get visitation rights. It was sad that a man who wanted to be in his child's life was being denied. At the same time, I was hoping that one day my girls' father would have a good relationship with them despite how little respect I had for him. It all seemed so unfair to the innocent victim, the children. Unfortunately, this was the second time Joey had suffered the loss of a relationship with a child.

Joey told me several months before we were married that he dated a girl briefly several years prior to our getting back together and that they'd had a child together. He recounted the painful story of how his ex-girlfriend informed him three years after they broke up that their brief relationship produced a child. The girl's boyfriend assumed the child was his. She told Joey that he couldn't be involved with their child because she didn't want to disrupt the child's life. He decided to honor her wishes and not put up a fight. I believe Joey was always bothered by this loss, and that it made him determined to be there for his other child, Porsche.

Joey and I had many things in common, but we also were very different in many ways. One thing was that Joey and I still had different religious backgrounds. But this time he didn't insist I become Muslim in order for us to be together as he had when we dated in college. We agreed to respect each other's religions and compromised on the celebration of holidays. For instance, the girls and I could celebrate Christian holidays such as Christmas and Easter, but without Santa Claus or the Easter Bunny. He, however, didn't want to celebrate any holidays. He was not a holiday person. He didn't even like celebrating birthdays. This was hard for me because these things were part of my childhood. Our compromise consisted of sticking to the truth when we celebrated religious holidays—Santa Claus and the Easter Bunny, after all, were fantasies. We also agreed that if we had children together they would be raised in the Sunni Muslim faith. At the time, I had no real objections to his religion. He believed in God and his Muslim practices were aligned with many of my religious morals. The only thing I wouldn't agree to was the Muslim practice of polygamy. I told Joey if he ever wanted another wife he would lose the one he had. He assured me that I was the only woman he wanted to marry.

A few months before I was remarried, Pete began paying child support again. His life became more stable and he occasionally visited the girls, even though he broke many promises to them by not showing up. I never forbade his calls or visits because I didn't want to deny them contact with their father, despite feeling the constant letdowns were hurting them. Soon after I remarried, Pete lost his job and got my child support reduced to thirty-eight dollars a week for two children. I was never offered the opportunity to contest the decision and as time went on, he stopped paying child support all together. I wasn't surprised but I was very disappointed.

We survived the storms surrounding our children and had a beautiful wedding. The night before, Joey spent a quiet night at home instead of having a bachelor party. Alicia spent the night with me. The morning of our wedding, Mrs. Peters, my former mother-in-law, came over to give me her blessings and videotaped our morning wedding preparations. Mrs. Peters said that she always liked Joey and thought he was very nice. My girls and I went to a hair salon the morning of July third and got spiral curls. The girls wore my favorite, purple-and-pink dresses. I wore an off the shoulder, cream-colored, lace, tea-length dress. My mom made our wedding bouquets. Mrs. Peters offered to keep the girls after the wedding so that we could spend our honeymoon alone. My mom and her new husband Freeman, Dawn, and Alicia were all there at the house while we got ready. We took pictures while putting on the final touches, and then started our caravan toward Vermont. My friend Dawn got separated from us, so we waited for her on the road. We didn't even realize how long we were looking for her, so we didn't think to call to let Joey know we were behind schedule. We were an hour late for the ceremony. When we finally got to our gazebo in Vermont, Joey said he was worried that I may have changed my mind.

It was a perfect day, warm and sunny, with a clear blue sky and a nice breeze blowing. We had a brief, yet memorable, ceremony that was videotaped, and we took many pictures before returning home to Massachusetts.

Joey's parents had planned an intimate gathering at their home that turned into a full-fledged party. All of their relatives cooked a huge, down-home spread. My mother made the wedding cake. There were tables with umbrellas and the yard was decorated in purple and white. It was absolutely beautiful. Family, friends, and neighbors came. Some of Joey's friends came by to "see who could get Joey to tie the knot." There was good music, good food, and good company. It couldn't have been a better day. Joey's brother Tony gave a traditional toast and Joey gave a beautiful speech after we cut the cake. He said that he didn't expect the outpouring of love and gifts for our quiet little ceremony and gathering but they all helped to make it "the happiest day of his life."

After the party, we left for our two-day honeymoon. We spent one night in a beautiful hotel and then went to New York City for the Fourth of July festivities. New York City had always been a favorite place of ours. Instead of a traditional, long honeymoon, Joey planned to take the girls and me to meet his grandmother and other family members in Mississippi after returning from New York City. This may not seem like a romantic honeymoon, but for someone like me who craved being part of a large family, it was blissful. It was also special that he included my girls. How many men would include their stepchildren on their honeymoon?

On our trip to Mississippi, I met Joey's brother Leonard and his wife, Joey's grandmother, and other extended-family members. When Joey told me that his grandmother loved me, I wanted to melt. His brother showed us around town and took us to New Orleans and to the beach in Gulfport, Louisiana. It was a great beginning to the rest of our lives. This time, I felt I had it all. Joey's family was wonderful. Two of his sisters and I were friends. His extended family welcomed me with open arms. He was loving and attentive to my girls and to me. My mother approved of Joey because he had some college education and was from an upstanding, hardworking, respectable family. His folks were great parents of six grown children and my mom knew they would be wonderful grandparents. My mother was happily remarried and she and I had a closer relationship. What more could I want?

I had a loving family with a good husband, great parents, two wonderful daughters, and caring in-laws. I felt guilty for wanting any more, but in the back of my mind I still wanted to find my birth mother. Over the years, I had started and stalled many searches for her. I contacted search agencies and then got depressed when I had no success. Once Joey hired US Search, an agency advertised on TV that guaranteed results. All we got was lists of hundreds of people with my birth mother's maiden name or a name close to hers. The thought of making calls to all those people and asking, "Are you my mother?" and then getting no results made me anxious. I preferred not to try, rather than to continue being disappointed.

For some reason I continuously misplace my adoption papers. I would get a burning desire to read the one-page letter given to my mother when she adopted me or the two-page letter Mrs. Bland wrote telling her about "Tanya's" likes and dislikes. I hunted furiously for those letters and when I couldn't find them, I got frustrated and tried to put it out of my mind. My mother supported my desire to search, but I felt guilty asking her too many questions. I finally decided that if we were to be reunited, my birth mother would have to find me. It became too much of a roller coaster ride. I tried to concentrate on my blessings.

Around this time, turmoil arose surrounding Joey's attempt to gain visiting rights to his daughter. He had to go to court, and Porsche's mother caused a lot of chaos. At my job, the management staff was being downsized, and I was expected to work weekends and holidays again, and assume more responsibility. My laid-back, exciting job was becoming much more stressful. Joey and I decided it was time for a change. I changed positions and became a pediatric visiting nurse. This job gave me more freedom and less stress, with no working weekends or holidays. We decided to use some of my vacation time to take a break before I started my new position. Pete's sister volunteered to watch the girls and we drove to Atlanta. Joey's cousin lived there and it was a place I had always wanted to visit.

I was excited about seeing the Martin Luther King, Jr. memorial and other historic sights. We were both happy about getting away from the drama at home. Joey also wanted to look up the daughter he wasn't able to claim as his own. She lived in Atlanta and her mother agreed to let us see her as long as we didn't say who we were. We went to visit her and met an adorable, shy, little girl who looked just like Joey. She had freckles and moles just like he and his mom. Joey's heart melted. I suggested that he buy her a ring so that she could have a lasting memento of him. Maybe one day she would know the truth and would know that Joey wanted to be a part of her life. We took photos so that we could have pictures of them together. The only photos we had of her were those that the child's grandmother occasionally sent Joey. At least he had this one opportunity to talk to and touch his little girl, even if she didn't know who he was.

It wasn't very long before our lives changed again. With the New Year, I discovered we would have a new addition to our family. I was pregnant. We were ecstatic. We would finally have a child together. Joey and I both wanted a son. He had two daughters and I had two daughters. I couldn't wait until we had our first ultrasound to find out the sex of our unborn baby. When the ultrasound technician told us it was a boy, Joey stood up and shouted *Allah Akbar*—God is great. I was excited. The girls were excited. Even my mom was excited. She always wanted a son, and now she would have a grandson. He became the "center of her universe" as she later referred to him.

Not too long before my delivery, I decided to insist on getting the child support that was due to my girls. I contacted Pete and he agreed to start living up to his financial responsibilities. The day after his first payment was due, I called him.

"Pete, this is Barbara. I didn't receive the thirty-eight dollars you promised to start paying me weekly for the girls. What's up?"

"I decided not to send it," he said very matter-of-factly.

"Why is that?" I said.

"I want to buy a boat. You have a job. You have been waiting all this time; you can wait a little longer. I'll pay when I can, after I buy my boat."

"So, a boat is more important than your daughters?" I said.

"I didn't say that. Look, you have a good job. You were able to take care of them when you were alone and now you are married again. You can work it out," he replied.

"You know, this isn't fair to me or to the girls. I shouldn't have trusted you. I should have notified the court that you weren't paying a long time ago."

"Well, you didn't," he said.

"Well, I should," I said.

"Go ahead and do it. I don't care. I'll pay you when I feel like it," he said before hanging up.

I was so angry that I decided to take him back to court. I filed the papers the very next day, and a court date was set. He was very angry when he received the papers summoning him to court for nonpayment of child support. He didn't believe I would go through with it.

When we had our day in court, he was even more angry and surprised by how the judge treated him. This judge showed him no mercy and sentenced him to six months in jail if he couldn't catch up on his payments immediately. Even though I was fed up with him, I actually felt bad for him as I watched them take him out of the courtroom in handcuffs. He was told he was in contempt and he would remain in jail until his debt was paid. They gave us another court date in six months to evaluate his status.

When his six-month sentence was up, the judge asked me if I wanted him locked up again until he paid his debt. As stupid as it sounds, I thought he'd learned his lesson and asked the judge to release him. While he was in jail, he became a Muslim. Muslims are taught the importance of caring for their families. He said he wanted to be a part of his children's lives both financially and emotionally and I wanted to believe him and give the girls an opportunity to see their father again. Joey tried to help him find work at a local cab company that was owned by Muslims. He came around for a while, visiting the girls, attending one of their swim meets, and giving us meager support checks. That was short-lived.

Shortly after getting out of jail, he moved out of state and stayed away for the remainder of their childhood so that he wouldn't have to pay child support or go back to jail. This period of time during and after his incarceration also put a strain on my relationship with his family. I thought that his family should have tried harder to give the girls the love and support they needed in their father's absence. Instead, they began to be less involved with them. This was especially hard on Brittany. The upcoming years would include many missed birthdays and holidays. They cared about the girls, but were overwhelmed with the stresses in their own lives and the lives of their other grandchildren and weren't able to be there for India and Brittany.

I felt terrible for the girls, but at least they were excited at the prospect of having a baby brother. We were all excited. As with my pregnancy with India, I chose to work up until delivery. As the time got closer, I became very tired. I was due at the end of September 1996, but I went into labor two weeks early. Joey became even more excited when I started labor.

We called my mother to come over and watch the girls when my labor began in the middle of the night. She was only two miles away so she arrived quickly, as Joey was helping me into the car. He sped so fast down State Street that I was afraid we would be pulled over by the police. Unlike my first two labors, this one was a breeze. I was checked into my birthing room and assigned to a nurse named Sandy that I knew from my days working at the hospital. My friend the epidural greeted me and I labored pain free for five hours as Sandy rubbed my feet and we talked about old times at Baystate Medical Center. I pushed our baby son, Joey Gowan, Jr., into the world with ease. Joey's mom nicknamed him JJ.

He was somewhat small, 6 pounds, 14 ounces, but he was strong and healthy. It was a happy and blessed day that I will always remember with joy. Joey shared the news of our first son's birth that afternoon when he went to pray at the mosque. India and Brittany woke up on Friday morning to the news from my mom, who they called Nana Miller, that they had a baby brother. My mother drove them to the hospital to see their brother before they went to school. They held him and studied him and couldn't wait for me to bring him home. I felt like our family was now complete. The Gowans were now a blended family with "yours, mine, and ours."

Brittany had just turned seven and had her birthday party scheduled at Inter-skate-91 for the next day. Joey picked up Porsche and went on with the party even though I was still in the hospital. They made Brittany's party special. Veronica had previously planned a baby shower for me on a date that ended up being two days *after* my son's early arrival. I was discharged from the hospital and went with baby in tow to my shower. Veronica, Dawn, and another friend, Greer, helped with the celebration. All my friends were there. I was especially happy that my mom's old friend, "Auntie June," was there. By the time I got home I was overjoyed and exhausted. I felt so special and loved. It was the best feeling, and once again I was on top of the world.

When I returned to work, a neighborhood lady who'd watched my girls after school volunteered to be JJ's daycare provider. I loved Mrs. Lewis and knew she would take good care of him. Within a few months, however, she was no longer able to run her daycare. She was preparing to move. I was at a loss for a babysitter. Joey's mom couldn't watch JJ, and my mom always told me she didn't like taking care of little babies. She loved them but enjoyed them more when they were "big enough to wash their own behinds and express their needs with words, not by crying." When I became a pediatric nurse, she didn't understand how I could take care of infants and young children. I didn't dare ask her.

To my surprise, my mother volunteered to come to my house to watch JJ until I could find someone else. This decision changed her forever. She had been just as strict and firm with my girls as she was with me. Nana Judy, Pete's mom, was the more fun grandmother. She bought toys and played with them. Nana Miller, my mom, bought savings bonds or practical gifts and did more talking with the girls than playing. I couldn't imagine my mom lasting more than a week caring for JJ. Much to my surprise, she fell absolutely, head-over-heels in love with him. She looked forward to seeing him everyday. She cooked dinner for us and played with JJ all day. Some days when I came home they would be curled up on the couch taking a nap. JJ must have been the son my mother always wanted. He warmed her heart more than I was ever able to do. He also looked exactly like I did when I was a baby, which may have been part of the attraction.

My mother told me not to get another babysitter. She didn't want JJ with anyone but her. Everyone saw that she was not only nurturing to JJ, but she also began to be the same way with everyone else. Something about her had changed. She was happier, sweeter, and that gruff exterior seemed to fade away. It is amazing what the love of a child can do for a person. She bought Barney toys for JJ and started buying the girls more fun toys along with their more practical gifts.

This new mom of mine was a breath of fresh air. She was thrilled that Joey's parents were a part of my life and hers, too. She loved them dearly. Joey's mom was very sweet, kind, and soft-spoken. She included my mom in their family celebrations. Joey's father, JW, was more like my mom. They told off-color jokes and were loud and gregarious. JW told my mother that my girls were his grandkids, not his step-grandkids, and he loved them the same as the rest of his grandkids. He also said he loved me just like his daughters. My mom knew how important that was to me, being accepted so unconditionally. Joey's father asked me to call him Dad, which, of course, I did without reservation. When my mother spent time with her new in-laws, she was comfortable about being away from me, because she knew that I was in good hands with my in-laws and with Veronica and Dawn's families.

Joey didn't want me to go back on birth control. Not that we wanted more children right away, but we decided to let God be in charge. It must have been

God's plan for us to have another child. I found out I was pregnant right around JJ's first birthday. I always wanted a big family and now I was going to have one.

This pregnancy was my hardest. I was older and was carrying more weight since the pregnancies were so close together. I had a fall that caused a bleeding scare and was more tired at work. We found out we were having another boy. Joey and I were both very happy about that. The big girls had each other and now the boys would have each other, and Porsche would have them all.

In the midst of my excitement, I soon found out from one of the ultrasounds that our new baby might have Down syndrome. I became worried. I knew how hard it was to care for healthy children, let alone a child with special needs. Joey comforted me by reminding me that we both had jobs that required us to care for people with problems. Who would be better able to care for him than we? He would be our child and we would love him no matter what. My love for Joey grew even more that night. Calm came over me. I didn't worry about it any more.

I became so exhausted near the end of the pregnancy; I asked my obstetrician if he could induce my labor early. He agreed, and I had the best three nights' sleep that weekend that I had had in a long time. Monday morning, Joey took a picture of my last pregnant belly. We knew this would be the last baby. While I was getting ready to leave for the hospital, my water broke. It was going to be John's birthday whether or not my labor was induced. We named our baby John Wesley Harold Gowan after both of our fathers. We wanted their names carried on as Brittany carried on Michelle's. My mother was delighted that John's middle name was Harold after my father, the love of her life. I wished for a brown baby with freckles like his father.

Veronica brought the girls to the hospital to witness John's birth. They were old enough to appreciate the experience and this would be our last baby. The first thing I asked Veronica was, "Does he look healthy?" She said, "Yes." He was my biggest baby at 8 pounds, 15 ounces, and he was perfectly healthy. My friend Greer, who was my children's pediatrician, confirmed that he was a healthy baby with brown skin and freckles everywhere. I remember saying, "I didn't mean *that* many freckles!"

After returning home from the hospital, I was concerned about being able to handle taking care of four children at home, and five, with Porsche, on the weekends. I knew it would be harder but I got what I'd always wanted—a big family. I was more tired, was suffering with pain from my tubal ligation, the pain from the spinal, breast-feeding an infant, and caring for a toddler. Also, the comfort of knowing my mother was at home to care for JJ was over. She was now 71 years old and had a husband at home who needed her more as he was having health problems. She was also still working part time as a nurse. She told me that she worked because she always wanted to have enough money to do the things she wanted and have enough savings to take care of herself if she ever grew ill. She said it was important to keep a nest egg, just in case.

My mother made me promise that if I couldn't take care of her with minimal outside assistance that I would place her in a nursing home. I told her I couldn't keep that promise. She wanted me to know, while she was cognizant enough to make proper decisions that she didn't want to ruin my life by having to take care of her. She didn't want to be a burden to anyone. She said that if she was in a nice nursing home and I checked on her daily to make sure she was getting proper care, she would be fine. She thought that when she got old she might try to convince me to move her into my home, but that I should not listen to her then. I told her to stop worrying about "what if" and live for right now. She took care of me all of my life and I would take care of her. That is how it ought to be. As much as I enjoyed my mom caring for JJ in our home, I knew it was time for her to have a break. She probably would never have stopped caring for him until he went to kindergarten if I hadn't had another baby. She knew she could never take care of two. One was hard enough.

Our pediatrician recommended a sweet, Hispanic woman named Rosa to take care of John and JJ. She became our boys' guardian angel. She and her family were kind and loving and treated them like family. My boys grew attached to them and to the other children in her daycare.

Once again, loving and caring people surrounded us. The girls loved having little brothers. India was especially close to JJ. Our neighbor, Jessica, fell in love with John. Brittany was the playmate for all of the little kids. My mom used to call John "little black Harold" after my dad; and of course, JJ was her heart. Those two had a bond closer than most mothers and their children. Unfortunately, she soon didn't get to spend as much time with her grandchildren. She had to spend more with her husband as he recovered from heart surgery. She was now worried that she would lose another husband. We tried to give her support and encouragement during this difficult time. I reminded her that both of us needed to "think about the beauty still around you and be happy" as Anne Frank wrote. Tomorrows are never guaranteed and we often miss many opportunities to be happy by dwelling on the past or worrying about the future.

John and JJ

7

Orphaned Again

For everything there is a season, and a time for every purpose under heaven.

—Ecclesiastes 3:1

One evening in November 1998, just before Thanksgiving, my mom was calling home from work to check on her husband, Freeman. She got no answer, so she asked me to go to her house and check on him. I drove to her house assuming he was asleep watching television. When I arrived, I walked into the den, and the TV was on just like I had suspected. Freeman was lying on the couch and looked like he was sleeping. I called his name but he did not answer. I walked over to him and called his name again. No answer. I reached out to touch him and he felt a little cold. I immediately felt a wave of panic come over me. He wasn't breathing and I felt no pulse. Even though I am a nurse and know what to do in this situation, this was different. He was family.

Freeman appeared to be dead. I was frightened. I called 911 and then attempted to do CPR, even though I suspected it would be useless. I tried and tried to no avail. When the paramedics arrived, they told me he had probably died long before I arrived. I think I knew that in my heart, but hearing it from someone else was reassuring. I felt bad, at first, thinking I should have tried harder to save him.

Now I knew I had to call my mom and tell her. I walked into the kitchen and tried to compose myself. I knew I needed to muster up all my strength to calmly tell her that her fears were not unfounded. She had just lost another husband. When she answered the phone at her job, I hesitated at first, because I knew what I was about to tell her was going to cause her a great deal of pain. I tried to comfort her by telling her that it looked like he died peacefully in his sleep and that we would get through this together.

It is hard to put into words how difficult it is to find someone you love dead. Freeman had recovered from his surgery and seemed to be doing better. Thanksgiving was right around the corner and once again my mother would have to deal with death and heartbreak during the holiday season. She was devastated. She was 71 years old and alone again. She became anxious and depressed. She used to say, "You come into this world alone and you die alone." Despite this saying, and the fact that she usually enjoyed being alone, she couldn't bear being alone in her house after Freeman died. Every night for about two months, India and I took turns sleeping overnight with her. Most of the time, she didn't want to talk. She just didn't want to be alone. Sometimes we heard her quietly crying in her room. We felt helpless seeing her in pain and knowing that there was nothing we could do to make it any better except to be there for her.

Freeman and my mother were looking forward to an eleven-day cruise that they had planned for January 1999. After losing him, she was at a loss for what to do about the cruise. Finally, she called and asked me to go with her. I had never been on a cruise and wanted to go with her but was afraid to leave JJ because he was so attached both of us. She decided we would take JJ with us.

Mom, JJ, and I departed for our cruise that January. Aside from early seasickness and the fact that Freeman's death was still fresh in our minds, we made the best of it. My mom was depressed, anxious, and sometimes claustrophobic during the cruise. The few times I was able to relax were sandwiched between taking care of my mom and taking care of my son. Parents expect to care for their children but children don't often think about having to care for their parents, especially when the parent has always been strong and independent. It was truly heartbreaking to see her so helpless and depressed.

JJ, on the other hand, was happy during the cruise because he got so much individual attention from each of us. He liked the pool, the playroom, and the great food. We traveled to the islands of St. Thomas, St. Kitts, Barbados, Trinidad, and Aruba. There was a winter storm back home in Massachusetts while we were away, and the kids were home because school was cancelled. As much as I missed my husband and my other children, I must admit I was happy to avoid the terrible weather. I enjoyed 90-degree temperatures, getting a great winter tan, and being able to spend quality time with my mom and my son.

This was my first experience with being exposed to so many different cultures in such a short period of time. We mingled with the locals and toured the islands. We got a personal tour of St. Thomas from one of Veronica's friends, who lived there. He took us to the top of a mountain, where we got the most beautiful views of the ocean and countryside. The clear blue waters were hypnotizing. After that trip, I knew that travel would become one of my lifelong passions.

I was amazed to learn how other cultures live. It was also nice to see the subtle differences on each of the islands and to be in places with all brown-skinned people. The only place I didn't like was Aruba. The people there were not as helpful and friendly as on the other islands. When I asked one lady how to use the phone to call home, I was asked where I was from and if I spoke Spanish. I told her I was from the United States and I didn't speak Spanish. After finding out that I was not from the island, she told me that she couldn't help me. I was shocked. I was unable to find anyone else to help me call home. One of the tourists I spoke with about my troubles calling home told me that she thought that those from Aruba traced their ancestors to South America and that the people from the other islands we visited traced their ancestors to Africa. I also was told that some of the people from Aruba trace their ancestry to the Netherlands. Perhaps that explained why she wanted to know about my ethnic background. It appeared that people all over the world judge others by their color and ethnicity. I thought it happened only in the United States. Once again, I was naïve.

The night that we returned home from our cruise, Veronica and my children planned a surprise "Welcome Home" party for us. My mother, however, had been feeling sicker and sicker during the journey home. By the time we reached Bradley International Airport, she said she needed to go to the emergency room. She was having difficulty breathing. I didn't know if it was anxiety or her asthma, but she needed to be seen by a doctor. The physician at the hospital who examined her admitted her for further testing. They later explained that her asthma and heart condition were the cause of her constant shortness of breath and discomfort. By the time I arrived home, the party atmosphere was gone. I appreciated their efforts, but I was physically and emotionally exhausted. Everyone was excited to see me and I received lots of hugs and kisses from the girls. I couldn't wait to go upstairs and see my little John. He was in his crib with my mother's friend, Miss Alice, by his side. At first it seemed as if he didn't recognize me. I called out his name and played the "catch a little mouse" game that my mom played with me and I played with all of my kids. When I started the game, he almost jumped out of the crib. Traveling is great, but there is no place like home.

As time went on, my mom grew accustomed to widowhood again and began to spend more time with us. She became much closer to the girls. They shared their deepest secrets with her. She told them that they could talk to her about anything and she would be their confidante. She taught them lessons about life without her former hard exterior and gruff approach. I was happy that they were all getting closer. She also began to travel and socialize with her friends again.

I, too, was able to spend more time with my family around this time. I left my job as a visiting nurse and became a school nurse so I would have more time off with my children. By the fall of 1999, family was more important to me than my career. I started working at New Leadership Charter School. It was a predominantly minority school that was led by our local Urban League. It was a perfect match for me. I felt at home there and began to feel I had everything I needed in my life again. I settled into my new job a month before my birthday.

My thirty-sixth birthday was one I will never forget. I had lost all of the weight from my two pregnancies. Things were great with my family. John was a happy baby and followed JJ around everywhere. The girls seemed less upset about their father's absence, and were doing well in school. Porsche was able to come over more often and the stressful situation with her mother was lessening. My mom was also feeling better. I came home from getting my hair done for my birthday and was waiting for some friends to come over when my mother showed up with a cake and ice cream. Everyone sang "Happy Birthday" to me and we thoroughly enjoyed my mother's unexpected visit. This was a big surprise because my mother never made a big deal out of birthdays like I did. We took a nice picture together and I told her how much she meant to me and how happy I was that we had grown so close over the last few years.

My mother was in a good mood that day and was looking forward to her trip to North Carolina to visit her family. When it was time to take her to the airport, Joey asked me if I wanted him to take her since it was very early in the morning. I told him I wanted to drive her myself. I am now very happy that I did. We had a nice talk on the way to the airport. She told me how proud she was of me and how happy she was that I was married to Joey. She loved his family and she was happy that I finally got everything I wanted.

She enjoyed her visit with her family in North Carolina, but she got sick while she was there and decided that the next time her family saw her would be when they came to Massachusetts. She wasn't going south again. She was able to see her Aunt Annie again which meant a lot to her. She was able to reminisce with many of her old friends. We spoke on the phone often during her trip, and she said she was looking forward to coming home. She told me that she knew it may be her last time going south, and she felt that she'd seen everyone she needed to see. One of her friends wanted to pick her up from the airport, so she told me not to change my schedule in order to pick mom up. When my mother got home, she called to say that she had had a good trip, was feeling better, and would see me the next day.

I remember that next day so clearly. It was Election Day 1999. After work, I voted then I went to the YMCA for my daily hour of exercise before picking up the boys from Rosa's house. The clocks had just been turned back from daylight saving time and when I left the gym, I noticed how dark it was. When I arrived home, India and Brittany told me that my mom had just left our house. She came by to visit with them. India made her some tea while she watched videos with her and my goddaughter, April. The girls laughed at the critical comments my mom made about some of the singers in the BET videos. She left and told the girls, "Tell your mom to call me when she gets home. I want to see her and my boys!"

It was less than five minutes after I got home that the telephone rang. I thought it was my mom checking to see if I got home yet.

"Hello," I said as I was anticipating my mom's voice on the other end of the phone.

"Hi, may I speak with Barbara Gowan please?" said an unfamiliar female voice.

"This is she."

"This is Baystate Medical Center calling. Your mother, Thelma Miller, has just arrived by ambulance. We would like you to come to the hospital's emergency room as soon as possible."

"You must be mistaken. My mother just left my house a short time ago and she was fine."

"Mrs. Gowan, your name was listed as her closest relative in case of an emergency."

"Why is she there?" I asked.

"It appears that your mother may have had an asthma attack or a heart attack and the paramedics have tried to stabilize her condition. Can you get to the hospital as soon as possible?"

"I'm on my way," I said, with a million thoughts going through my head.

"Mrs. Gowan?"

"Yes."

"Could you bring someone with you when you come?"

I don't even remember responding. Her last question frightened me. That terrible, familiar sense of panic came over me once again. It was the same feeling I had when I saw Freeman in the den and when Michelle's boyfriend called to tell me that she died. I tried to appear calm in front of the kids because I didn't want to upset them but I was far from calm when I called for India to come to where I was standing.

"India, I need you to stay here to watch the boys. I have to go to the hospital."

"Why? What's wrong?" she asked.

"Nana is sick and in the emergency room. I need to check on her."

"Oh, no," she said, and started to cry.

"Don't cry, India. I'll call you as soon as I see Nana. OK?"

"OK, mommy."

"Mommy, can I come with you?" Brittany asked.

"OK, but we have to hurry," I said as I walked to the door.

I called Joey from the car and asked him to meet me at the hospital. I was driving down Sumner Avenue approaching the highway when Joey's mother called and asked me what was going on with my mom. I thought to myself, "How did she know?" When we arrived at the emergency room, I began asking questions about my mom and no one would give me a direct answer. Finally I asked, "Did she die?" I only remember someone simply replying "yes." They then took me to a room to meet with someone from their bereavement team. I knew the drill. I knew the process. I had been the comforting nurse to many families experiencing loss on our pediatric unit in the past. Now I was on the receiving end.

My mother died on November 2, 1999. That was the greatest loss of my life. Just one year before, I was comforting her after the loss of her husband. Now I needed comfort and had to deal with the loss of my mother. I was 36 years old and felt like a little child again. I was motherless and fatherless and felt hopeless. The doctors said they thought my mother came home and had an asthma attack, which then triggered a heart attack. She was the one who called 911. When they found her on the floor in her bedroom, bleeding from her fall to the ground, she still had her inhaler in her hand. The ambulance staff worked hard trying to revive her all the way to the hospital, but they couldn't save her. My worst nightmare came true. My mother was gone. I wanted to die myself at that moment. How could I live without her? My dad was gone. Freeman was gone. Michelle was gone. Now, my mother was gone. I felt alone in the world and abandoned again. I felt like an orphan. It would be yet another sad holiday season.

Brittany and I went in to see her. She looked so peaceful, but I didn't want to let her go. I kept stroking her hair. As with Michelle, her hair seemed to be the only thing that felt alive and real. Joey came in and we all said goodbye for the last time. The pain of losing a parent cannot be described. Part of me died with them. I was sad again that I didn't have any siblings that could share some of our memories. I felt like all of our memories died when they died. Who could I reminisce with about my childhood? Who would laugh with me at the private jokes only we shared?

I thought about the last time I had seen her. It was our ride to the airport when she went to North Carolina. For some reason, I remembered that when she got out of the car, she asked me if I had any mints so I offered her a brand new box of Altoids. She smiled and said, "I only wanted one!" I told her, "Just keep the whole box, you may need them later." She gave me a big grin and said, "Thanks." When they gave me her personal belongings at the hospital, that box of Altoids was still in her purse.

My mother talked to me at length on many occasions about what to do when she died. She told me where all of her valuables were hidden and "to take care of business" before shedding one tear. She knew how emotional I was. She always said that she wanted to be cremated; she didn't want to be "on display." She also didn't want me to "spend one red cent" on flowers after she was gone. She would always say it was more important to give her live plants and flowers for her garden while she was able to enjoy them than when she was gone. Although she had told me these things, I was still so afraid of doing the wrong thing when it came to her final arrangements that I called her closest friends to ask their advice. I always had my mother to turn to if I ever needed anything. Who was I to turn to now? I was an emotional wreck. She said that she knew I would have a difficult time when she died and she wanted to make it easier for me. That is why she made her own burial arrangements and bought a plot next to my dad. I called all of her closest friends, near and far, to let them know she was gone. I was tired and emotionally drained, again wishing I had siblings or aunts and uncles around to help me with all that I had to do. I always felt uncomfortable asking anyone for help and I didn't want to start now. Luckily, I had great friends who came forward and volunteered to help me whether I asked or not. My mother didn't want a wake or a funeral, so I arranged for a quiet graveside service with a priest, as she had wanted. Friends and family came out to the graveside on that very cold and dismal day to say their goodbyes to my mom. Brittany and I wrote letters to my mother but were too filled with grief to read them aloud ourselves. My friend Dawn volunteered to read the letters for us. They went like this:

Dear Mommy,

I'm writing this letter to you because I miss you so much and am hurting so much and wish I could've said goodbye to you. I wish I could've told you how much I love and need you and how proud I am that you were my mom. I am happy that you saw your family down south and that you had a good day with your friends and that you visited with India and Britt before you went with God. I only wish I could've seen you one last time and am sad that JJ and John didn't say goodbye. I told JJ tonight that you went to heaven to be with God and that he could talk to you whenever he wanted to. He drew you the picture on the back of this letter and wanted me to trace his hands and he said goodbye and said, "I love you Nana." Believe it or not, John, "little black Harold" as you used to call him was looking at your picture and JJ said, "It's Nana" and John said, "Nana" for the first time. I promise I'll make them remember you and remind JJ that he was the center of your universe. India told me one day when she was mad at me that the older I get the more I get like you. At first I was mad because she meant I was being too strict or mean but now I take it as the best compliment because I love you so and hope you'll live on in me and my family. I'll always love you and miss you.

Your daughter "Barbie"

p.s. Brittany said "you never realize how much you love someone until they are gone" and it's true. I just wish I could've told you again how much I really loved you.

Dear Nana,

I miss you so much. I wish you were here. I cried for days and wished you would come back. You are my favorite grandma. You taught me right from wrong. You taught me how to talk to my mom. And you respect me. So I guess that's why I love you so much. I hope God takes good care of you.

Love,

Britt, Britt

P.s. say hi to grandpa, Freeman, and Michelle for me. I hope you're happy. Love you. Bye.

We were all overcome with grief. Brittany said that she never hurt so badly in all of her life. She was also sad to see Joey cry; she never saw him cry before.

My mother's old friend and neighbor, Alice, arranged to have a small gathering after the service in the social room at her building. Alice and her daughter Connie, my old childhood friend and neighbor, were a blessing to me during that time. They knew mom and me better than most, as we spent so much time together when we were younger. Connie volunteered to take my mom's dog home with her to Maryland to further lessen my burden. I spent time with all of the family and friends that came out that day but I was so emotionally drained that all I really wanted to do was to sleep the pain away. That is exactly what I tried to do, until the reality of all of the things I still had to do woke me from my slumber.

I had to take care of my mother's affairs. She had property in the South as well as her home in Massachusetts. This was the home I grew up in and the home where I had most of my childhood memories. It was also the home where she and her husband died. It was a daunting task, but I found comfort being around her things and being in my old house. I decided to replace many things in our house with furnishings from my mother's house. I needed to have her things with me permanently. She had a dining room table that was her pride and joy. It was one of the first things she bought when she married my dad. It had a punch bowl on it where she kept fruit. She also had an antique silver frame with my favorite photo of her in it. These are some of my most prized possessions that have a place of reverence in our home. To this day, we honor the many things in our house that were hers. The boys sometimes say, "Don't put your feet on Nana's coffee table" or "Be careful with Nana's picture." There are photos of my mom and dad in the house and we talk about them all the time. I don't ever want them to be forgotten.

That Thanksgiving I wanted to use my mother's dining room table that I had just moved into my house. We had a tradition of baking homemade piecrust with my mother's special recipe. I had some of her favorite recipes written down but many times I just called her up when I needed them. I put the sweet potatoes on to boil for her famous sweet potato pie and started looking for the sweet potato pie recipe. I couldn't find it. I searched frantically everywhere for it. Everyone thought I was going crazy. The recipe was lost and I couldn't call my mother to ask her for it! I called Joey's mom. She tried to calm me down by giving me a list of ingredients that she used. I knew hers was different. It was good, but I wanted my mother's. I could still imagine how it tasted. I played with the ingredients until it tasted like my mothers and wrote it down. I realized there were many things I would never get a chance to tell or ask my mom. With the help of great friends and family, I survived that holiday season. But I knew it would be a long time before I would feel joy again.

I had to finish taking care of my mother's affairs. In between working and taking care of my family, I went to my mother's house every weekend to sort through her things. The most difficult task was to clean up her bedroom. She spent her last moments there and there were reminders of the chaos that had ensued. I could still smell her. I imagined what her last moments were like. That was so difficult. I forced myself to picture her in more peaceful times, lying in her bed reading a book, as she did every night.

I couldn't throw anything away until I read or examined it for its importance. I looked at every book, every shoe, and every piece of paper before discarding it. People told me to get a big dumpster and throw all of those things away. I couldn't do that. My mother was a packrat who didn't believe in throwing anything away unless it had absolutely no value. I tried to conduct myself so my actions would honor my mom.

It took me six months to finish clearing out her house. It was a lot of work but it served as a healing process for me. By the time the house was empty I was ready to move on to the next stage of my healing. I made up care packages of mementos of my mom for all of her close friends. I saved her china and crystal to give to my daughters when they were older. They say God never gives you more than you can handle; and if He brings you to it, He'll bring you through it. I can attest to that. God brought me through that pain and I was comforted with the verse from Ecclesiastes that says, "For everything there is a season, and a time for every purpose under heaven." My mother's season was over. Her purpose was completed. It was time for me to grow up and fulfill the purpose of my own life.

PART III
Finding My Faith

8

Accepting the Truth

o o o o o o o o o o o o o o o o o o o o o o o o o o o o o o o o
Then you will know the truth, and the truth will set you free

—John 8:32

September 11, 2001, is a day that changed the lives of every American. I was in my office at New Leadership Charter School. Joey called and told me to turn on the news. I turned it on to see the Twin Towers of the World Trade Center in flames and then collapse one by one. It was surreal and I couldn't believe my eyes. The students were summoned to the auditorium and told about the disaster. I couldn't understand how or why it happened. Staff members were frantically calling their family members who lived near the Twin Towers to make sure they were OK. We later found out it was an act of terrorism. Joey and I had differing opinions about the attack and about the theology of our religious beliefs. This became an ongoing controversial topic of discussion in our home.

Islam teaches peace but it also teaches Jihad, which is interpreted differently by different individuals. In my opinion this kind of act is against God's will. Joey didn't agree with the attack but he understood how someone could be driven to it. He said that if someone were to attack our home and take over our property, he would retaliate just like the Muslims are doing in the Middle East to defend their land. He explained that since our country was allied with Israel, we were seen as enemies to Islam. I was appalled by the terrorist actions regardless of their religion or their motivation.

We discussed and debated this issue but we never were able to see eye to eye on it. It sounded ridiculous to me for him to try to explain and justify the attacks. I could not understand a religion that went against the basic laws of God in the Ten Commandments.

These discussions led me to an overwhelming need to seek God for myself. I decided to read the Bible cover to cover and allow the Holy Spirit to minister to me. It was time for me to learn about my God and seek the faith that I had been missing. I was like a little kid waking up every morning looking forward to learning more. Teachers at the school saw me reading the Bible and started conversations with me about the Word of God. I had never discussed religion with anyone at work before except Mr. Aleem who was our guidance counselor. I often talked to him about Islam for a better understanding of my husband's religion. He encouraged many interfaith meetings in the community and was himself married to a Christian.

When I told people about my quest for knowledge and understanding of the Bible, other Christians seemed to come out of the woodwork. I felt encouraged everyday. I constantly asked my Christian friends questions. I called Dana in Delaware and Veronica and we had Bible study over the phone. I learned more about Christianity in that two-and-a-half-month period than I did in all of my years in the Catholic Church.

When I finished the New Testament, I knew that I needed to find a church home. While I read the Bible, I listened to a CD by Howard Hewitt, called *The Journey*. It became one of my favorites. I initially fell in love with the more popular song *Say Amen*, but the title track would grow to hold the most meaning for me. It illustrated the parable in *Matthew 25*, which tells of gifts and talents given by the Lord. It discussed the importance of being faithful with the gifts you are given. The song asked the question, "What are you doing with your gifts (or talents) and what are you doing with your life?" It inspired me to want to make a difference and to use my gifts to glorify God. It is amazing how one song or one passage in the Bible can affect one's outlook on life.

As I read through the parables that Jesus used to teach lessons, I could feel myself changing. For example, I read in *Matthew 18* the parable of the servant who was forgiven his debt by his master, but then was unwilling to forgive a much smaller debt owed him by another and had the debtor thrown in jail. When his master heard of this, he said, "You wicked servant; I forgave you all that debt … should you not also have had compassion on your fellow servant just as I had pity on you?" When Jesus heard that the master sentenced this servant to torture, he said, "So my heavenly Father also will do to you if each of you, from his heart, does not forgive his brother his trespasses." Those words made me think. I often held grudges. I thought long and hard about anything anyone did to hurt me and "gave them a piece of my mind" afterward. Although I always tried to be understanding and looked for the best in people, I had a hard time with forgiveness. I knew that I wanted to be forgiven for my sins, and I realized at that moment that I had to forgive others.

I believe I gained good moral character from hearing about these parables as a child, but I don't think that they became part of my spirit until that fall of 2001. I recalled the parables about reaping what you've sown and having the faith of a mustard seed, but I didn't really fully understand what they meant until I read them again as an adult.

On one hand, this new insight helped my relationship with Joey as I began to forgive him for some of his past mistakes; but on the other hand, I had a hard time with some of the philosophies of his religion. One belief that was difficult for me to reconcile with was that Muslims say that Jesus was a prophet like Muhammad and not the Son of God. I read that a house divided will not stand and I was afraid our house would fall.

In my search for a church home, I visited my mother-in-law's church. It was nice, but I didn't feel it was the place for me. Joey and Veronica both mentioned a church that had an anointed pastor, Reverend Howard-John Wesley. I never heard of him or St. John's Congregational Church. Joey said he visited that same church prior to Pastor Wesley's arrival because Muslims are encouraged to learn about other religions. He often frequented different places of worship. I was not familiar with many black churches in our city. The church our neighbors, the Ayalas, attended with my girls, and the church the Peters, my former in-laws, attended were not typical black churches. I was a little nervous about going to a new and unfamiliar church, but I decided to visit it with Dawn's father since he attended St. John's regularly and invited me to go with him and his new wife. (Dawn's mother had died of cancer a few years earlier).

My fears were all unfounded. I knew many of the members and they greeted me with an inviting spirit and Christian love. It was a wonderful experience and one I will never forget. I knew right then and there that St. John's would be my church home. When I got home I told Joey I was going to join the church. Most people joined St. John's because of Pastor Wesley's preaching. When I visited, the assistant, Pastor Catherine, was preaching, but I still knew it was the place for me. It was the loving spirit of the church, not only the preached word that inspired me to join. I immediately felt I belonged there. I didn't want to walk down the aisle when they opened the doors to the church for new members. I decided to go to the church office the next day to join. I met with Pastor Catherine and she read Romans 10 to me, which says, "If you confess with your mouth the Lord Jesus and believe in your heart that God raised Him from the dead, you will be saved." I was so excited. I felt I now had a personal relationship with my

Savior and not just the religious teaching I had when I was younger. I always was seeking true faith and not just religious knowledge. I now had what I was searching for. I also found a church family that made me feel at home.

That next Sunday, I took the children to church with me. Pastor Wesley was starting a series called, "How are you going to celebrate Christmas?" He was as dynamic a preacher as I had heard. His message on the origins of Christmas was truly inspiring and educational. I knew this was the kind of preaching and teaching that Joey would respect.

Joey liked to seek information pertaining to religion. I believed in my heart that he followed Islam because he felt he found in it the truth he'd been seeking. I bought him a tape of Pastor Wesley's sermon and he enjoyed it. He respected Pastor Wesley's beliefs that celebrating Christmas with the Santa Claus myths that Europeans perpetrated was not part of Christianity. Pastor Wesley caused a furor in the church that day when he blurted out, "There is no Santa Claus." Many parents were upset with him because he instructed them to stop lying to their children about Santa Claus. He said, "Why lead children to believe a myth about a Santa Claus that they can't see, and then expect them to believe the truth about a God that they can't see?" The truth didn't upset our family since we never allowed our boys to believe in Santa Claus and the girls were older and knew Santa was not real.

Shortly after this, I met with Pastor Wesley and asked him all the questions I had about St. John's and Christianity. I asked him about the conflicts I was afraid of having at home because of our differing religious beliefs. In spite of telling Joey I would let my sons be raised in the Islamic faith, I now realized that I didn't want them to be raised Muslim. I expected a miracle or thought I would hear about a Bible verse that would show Joey the light. Pastor Wesley simply told me to let my actions draw my husband to Christ. He explained that no one could convince anyone else to follow any religion. I decided to follow his advice to demonstrate Christ-like behavior in my daily life, whether Joey noticed it or not.

Dana and Veronica helped me along my spiritual journey. Dana prayed that I would find a church home. I felt bad that Joey wasn't attending church with the rest of us, especially since I visited his mosque often in the past with him. I attended St. John's every Sunday. Dana said she knew I would be as passionate about my faith as I was about everything else. I had always been dedicated to being a good student, a good nurse, a good mother, a good friend, and a good wife. Now, I wanted to be a good Christian, too.

We alternated visits with our friends Dana and Dave (her husband) once or twice a year. The weekend before the King Holiday on one of their visits to our home, they wanted to visit St. John's. Joey decided to come along to see what all of the excitement we felt was about. He loved it! Over the next couple of months, he kept coming back. He also went to Bible study with me and learned about Christianity. His greatest discovery was that the promise made to Abraham from God was made to the descendants of Isaac (Jews and later Christians) and not to the descendants of Ishmael (Muslims).

On Palm Sunday 2000, our family sat in the basement watching the service on the big screen television, as was the case when the church building was crowded. Pastor Wesley's sermon was about Jesus calling Peter to walk out on water by faith. He called out to anyone in the congregation who was also willing to step out on faith and come to Christ. To my surprise, Joey walked up to the front of the aisle. I couldn't believe Joey joined, let alone in the basement while watching the sermon on the TV. The girls and I were so happy. The ushers took him upstairs and I could see Pastor Wesley come down from the pulpit in excitement to shake his hand. He had been ministering to Joey with his Christ-like love and welcoming spirit since Joey's first visit. We couldn't wait to tell his family. They were quite surprised and happy. India said she had been praying for Joey to become Christian. His parents and his brother, Tony, said they also had been praying that we would all be able to worship together one day. This was the happiest I had been since I lost my mother. I now believed our house, no longer divided, would stand.

My new relationship with God reminded me that prejudice is a sin. We need to see people the way that God sees us, regardless of color. Coming to terms with that reality is what helped heal my old wounds and deal with the contradictory feelings about self-identity and race that plagued me most of my life.

Some of the contradictory feelings probably came from the conflicting messages I received from my mother, and some from my own personal experiences with racism and discrimination. Some feelings were probably because I knew I was biracial. I was able to love my white friends who were so kind to me, but had reservations about "the man," the white establishment. It was as if "the man" was to be studied and emulated yet not trusted; but individuals could be loved and trusted. I learned this distrust from my mother. I was now unlearning it on my spiritual journey.

I wanted peace in every area of my life. I reached out to make peace with Mrs. Peters (whose relationship with us had become strained) and Porsche's mother. It felt good to try to make a fresh start. With God's word and the guidance of Pastor Wesley and the other ministers in the church, I felt as though we were all becoming better people and getting closer to God. I loved the fact that our entire family was worshipping together. My young daughters got excited about Pastor Wesley's style of teaching and preaching. He made analogies that all ages could relate to and was able to hold the children's attention.

Whenever people join St. John's, we pray over them. One reason we pray is because we know that when souls are won for Christ, the Devil goes to work and they may be tested in their new-found faith. We were no different. I was feeling on top of the world again. I felt at peace with everyone in my life. Joey, India, Brittany and I all got baptized together. We were indeed "new creatures." Like other times in my life when I felt life couldn't get any better, we began to experience new trials. Our new-found faith was being tested with new problems; this time it was with our children. However, we had our church family and our spiritual base to help us through.

India was now in middle school. She met a white boy, named Cliff; they were supposedly "just friends." He was a blonde-haired, blue-eyed boy that India found charming and handsome. India seemed to be more comfortable with her white friends, just as I had been at one point in my childhood. When she asked if she could go to Six Flags with Cliff, we suspected that they were becoming more than just friends. I was very fearful that she would be subjected to some of the same prejudices that I had suffered. I didn't mind her dating a white boy, but I told her that she needed to be sure he would accept her as well as her culture. I didn't want her to have to ever hear the "N" word. I also didn't want her to be ashamed of who she was.

India assured me that Cliff had friends of all races. He lived in a predominantly black neighborhood and he attended the school where I worked. He seemed like a nice boy and he treated India well. As time went on, however, we became concerned because they were getting too serious for middle school. Cliff went to church with us and I developed a friendship with his mother. That is probably why I waited so long to forbid the relationship. Their relationship was on again, off again. When they would break up, I tried to console India, as I remembered how hard it was for me when I went through heartbreak with my first boyfriend. I also remembered how unsupportive my mother was with me during that time.

After dealing with him for over a year, I finally told India that if she and Cliff broke up one more time, I would not allow her to see him again. As I suspected, they did eventually break up again. This time, Cliff became very emotional and punched a wall. This reminded me of Pete's jealousy, controlling behavior, and violence. I knew I had to protect her. One afternoon, Cliff came to my office at school, yelled at me, and told me I couldn't stop them from being together. He cursed at me and was very irrational. I made the mistake of not reporting the incident to the school authorities immediately. I thought it would be better to ask his mother to speak to him about his disrespectful actions. I was wrong; she screamed at me and defended his behavior. I realized I had to notify the school principal and I prayed about it to decide what steps to take next.

India's pediatrician advised me to file a restraining order against Cliff and I took her advice, knowing that my first priority was to protect my daughter. India became very depressed after that for about a year. She began to skip school and became very defiant. Cliff tried to contact her even with the restraining order, which caused more problems.

I didn't share with Joey all of the problems with India and Cliff's relationship. He didn't think India should be allowed to have a boyfriend in the first place. My mother allowed me to have boyfriends, with close supervision, so I didn't think there was anything wrong with it. We had very different philosophies and I think it is difficult to determine the right thing to do in every situation. I also didn't want to strain his relationship with India. By this time the girls' relationship with Joey had changed, which created other problems.

India and Brittany thought Joey treated them differently than he treated Porsche. Neither Joey nor I ever hit or yelled at Porsche, no matter what she did. I didn't think it was my place to correct her and I think he didn't want Porsche upset with him since she didn't live with us. He thought my daughters should be punished and "whipped" for every disrespectful comment or offense. He didn't, however, feel that way when Porsche misbehaved. She was exempt from punishment. We talked about the difficulties of being stepparents. Children don't always bond with their stepparents the same way that they do with parents. Knowing this, I went the extra mile with Porsche and thought Joey should do the same with my daughters. He said that he loved all of the kids the same and he believed he treated them all the same. Everyone, including his parents, saw otherwise. We even had family meetings with his parents to try to work things out in this area.

I believe it is easier for parents to have a more natural, parent-child relationship with children they have known since birth than ones that come in the package deal of a marriage. That is why I went the extra mile with Porsche, knowing this is the first step to making a stepchild feel loved and accepted. Step parenting and raising adopted children seemed very similar to me. Both stepchildren and adopted children are not family by blood but still deserved to be loved and accepted just the same. Because Joey said he didn't think he treated them differently, he didn't feel the need to change anything.

Other issues that I tried to deny also became undeniable. We began to have family difficulties because of my husband's spending habits and desire for marijuana. I always knew he smoked, but thought it was only once in a while since he didn't do it in my presence. Marijuana doesn't have the stigma that other drugs do. I even tried it myself. It is often compared with alcohol. He didn't drink so I thought it wasn't a big deal. I realized after several years that he didn't just do it once in a while, and that it was a major problem.

I began to see how it affected his moods and judgment. He made irrational financial decisions. For example, he loved cars and bought them on the spur of the moment without having them checked out. We had ten cars in the first seven years we were married. I later realized that was a symptom of his addiction. He had a hard time making good decisions and often couldn't focus on one thing at a time. He was otherwise a good man. He didn't hang out in the clubs, and spent most of his free time at home and seemed to value his family. He wasn't jealous or abusive like my first husband. He even tried to quit smoking marijuana. He abstained for short periods of time and then would start again. He felt guilty and made promises but couldn't keep them.

We took our problems to the church in prayer. Constant prayer from my church family had brought Joey to Christ in only three months. I knew that prayers could heal our family, including my daughter India. She had always been an honor student and now, for two marking periods, her grades slipped. The Lord is faithful and it is written in *Matthew 7:7*, "Ask and it will be given to you; seek and you will find, knock and the door will be opened to you." I asked and had faith and God healed her from her depression. The next year she got straight A's and finished the year with a 3.5 grade point average. She was back on track. We also prayed for Cliff, but he continued to have problems. We were glad that at least he was out of India's life. We also prayed for God's help with Joey's problems.

In 2002, Joey and I began meeting with Pastor Wesley for spiritual guidance. We were also looking for something to read between our meetings. Dana recommended *The Purpose Driven Life*. Joey and I read a chapter a day as was recommended. It changed our lives. We learned that everyone's life has purpose and that people often let materialism, pride, careers, or other things block the true purpose. The first chapter says, "It's not about you. The purpose of your life is far greater than your own personal fulfillment, your peace of mind, or even your happiness … if you want to know why you were placed on this planet, you must begin with God. You were born by His purpose and for His purpose."

The second chapter began with "You are not an accident. Your birth was no mistake or mishap, and your life is no fluke of nature. Your parents may not have planned you, but God did." I felt like the author was talking to me. These words in the first two chapters made me realize I wasn't a "mistake." I was meant to be here. I just needed to understand my purpose. It went on to explain that we were created for God's pleasure, for God's family, to become like Christ, for serving God, and for a mission. We read the forty chapters in forty days and wanted to share our experience with everyone we knew. I testified about the impact it made on our lives when I attended prayer service. I decided to give the book to most of my friends and family, including Porsche's mother.

By this time, Porsche's mother was in a stable relationship. I thought that since she and I were both in a better place, we could reconcile the differences between our families. I realized that it took two people to argue and I had to be responsible for my part. I apologized to her for any harmful words I had spoken to her and tried to begin anew in this area of my life.

Another book that continued to make a difference in my life was *Codependent No More*. A case study of one man quoted him saying, "Give me a room full of women, and I'll fall in love with the one with the most problems ... Frankly they are more of a challenge." Another woman in the book said to her therapist, "All I know is nursing and I'm sick of taking care of people. My family and friends think I am a tower of strength. Good ol' dependable Patty. Always there. Always in control. Always ready to help them. The truth is I'm falling apart, very quietly but very certainly ... I even feel guilty about coming to see you." This woman sounded like me. I learned through reading this book that this common thread runs through all stories of codependence. I could see that common thread in all of my major relationships. One had a problem with alcohol, one with cocaine, and one with marijuana. Subconsciously I picked people I thought I could help. I actually thought it was my job to help them.

One incident with Porsche pointed out to me how my "helping" may have been related to my codependency. I asked a coworker of mine to pick Porsche up to take her to school every day since Porsche's mother didn't want to walk her to school, and I agreed to bring her home after school. One day in a bad snowstorm, my coworker was unable to pick her up so I volunteered to go and get her. To my utter amazement, her mother said she hated me always trying to help. I thought since we had made amends that she appreciated my help, especially since she didn't want to get up and bring her to school every day even though she wasn't working. I realized it was time for me to stop trying to rescue Porsche, too. That was her mother's job. My feelings were hurt, but I didn't say anything because I was in a different place now, and wanted to keep the peace. One of the ministers at St. John's pointed out to me that I was driving myself crazy trying to help everyone else and that just because I was trying to do the right thing that didn't mean anyone had to appreciate it. He said that I needed to start taking care of myself and stop worrying about everyone else. That really woke me up. Sometimes the truth hurts, but it will set you free.

As time went on I became an avid reader. I read Joyce Meyers' *In Pursuit of Peace*. The author, who is a minister, talked about finding true peace using twenty-one peacekeepers. They were divided into sections regarding being at peace with God, being at peace with oneself, and being at peace with others. This book changed how I was living my life. It referenced the Serenity Prayer, which was also cited in the codependency book. It seems so simple but it made me realize how I needed to live.

God grant me the Serenity to accept the things I cannot change, Courage to change the things I can, And the Wisdom to know the difference.

Meyers says that a life without peace might be the result of trying to change something that cannot be changed. Our job is to pray, and trust that God is totally and completely just. We want God to change our circumstances but He is more interested in changing us than in changing our situations. She said that we would experience peace in our personal lives when we stop trying to do things ourselves and wait for God to deliver, heal and save us, as He wants to do. I realized that we gain a right relationship with God through complete surrender to Him in every area of our lives and through repentance of our sins. The book gave practical, bible-based ways to attain peace in life. It was another book that I gave to many friends and family members.

I realized I couldn't change a lot of the things in my life. I couldn't change the circumstances of my birth or Porsche's. I couldn't make Pete be the loving and devoted father he used to be. I couldn't make anyone like or love my children. I couldn't make my husband stop smoking marijuana any more than I could make Pete stop using cocaine.

Also while reading *In Pursuit of Peace*, I realized I had to rid myself of the things Meyers called "peace stealers." For me that included my "helping." I decided the previous year to stop helping Porsche get back and forth to school, since her mother hated it and I had become more aware of my codependent, rescuing behavior. However, Joey didn't understand the change in my behavior. He expected the rescuing to continue. That next year, Porsche's mother still had not made arrangements for her transportation to and from school. This time, Joey wanted India, who was now seventeen, with a job and a car, to pick Porsche up from school even though her mom was at home and not working. I realized then and there that the enabling needed to stop. There was no reason for India to be responsible for Porsche's transportation when no one in her own household would do it. We needed to stop "fixing" things for good.

The other peace stealers in my life were my problems with family, belonging, loyalty, and trust. My beginnings seem to have been one big lie—from an altered birth certificate to a changed name. I craved family, honesty, and loyalty, but my life had been riddled with loss, lies, and infidelity. Trying to overcome these things became my weakness.

I finally surrendered and tried to rid myself of all of the "peace stealers" in my life and focused on trusting in God instead of worrying and "fixing." It is important to learn lessons when going through trials and tribulations. If not, the same mistakes will be repeated. I realized that when I stopped worrying about India and asked God to help, she was healed. When I gave Joey's addiction to God, Joey started a recovery process by going to meetings and counseling, although it was short-lived.

I began to spend more time focusing on my blessings instead of dwelling on my problems. I had a lot to be thankful for. I tried to stop worrying about pleasing others and do my best to please God. That was the best decision I ever made. Meyers also talked about trusting God. She cites two of my favorite scriptures: *Proverbs 3:5-6* "Trust in the Lord with all your heart and lean not on your own understanding; in all your ways acknowledge Him, and He will make your paths straight;" and *Philippians 4:6-7* "Do not be anxious about anything, but in everything, by prayer and petition, with thanksgiving, present your requests to God. And the peace of God, which transcends all understanding, will guard your hearts and your minds in Christ Jesus."

I felt like I was growing spiritually every day. Pastor Wesley teaches our congregation to be obedient to God in every area of our lives in order to receive blessings. I thought I was being obedient. I prayed every day, went to church every Sunday and to Bible study every Tuesday. I taught Children's Church on Sundays and gave money to the church. However, I had never heard about tithing, so this was an area where I was not obedient. I was very skeptical about churches that had many collection plates and repeatedly asked for money. The first time I went to St. John's I noticed that this didn't happen. Guests are asked to give an offering if they chose, but the church was supposed to be supported primarily from the tithes and offerings of its members.

After a series of teachings about money management and tithing, Joey and I decided we would try to be obedient to the teachings on tithing, or giving ten percent of earnings. We learned that tithing brings blessings. They are not always financial blessings, but blessings nevertheless. We stepped out on faith, began to tithe, and the blessings showed up. Twice, during times of need, I was notified about unclaimed property from my mother's estate, years after she died. Joey and I were both blessed with unsolicited job offers. I was also blessed with the support of many people in my church. I was feeling more at peace than I had ever felt before, despite the trials and tribulations I had to endure in my life. These blessings are immeasurable. Most important, I finally had the faith in God that I always wanted. I would never have been able to buy the peace and comfort that I began to feel. It is given only through God by the indwelling of the Holy Spirit. During the 2003 holiday season, I finally was able to accept how blessed I was with a loving church family and with wonderful friends. Even though Veronica's family treated me like a member and included me in their family gatherings, I often felt insecure. Sometimes I thought they felt sorry for me because my parents were gone, or were being nice to me only because I was Veronica's friend.

My own personal issues of lack of belonging and rejection prevented me from seeing their sincere feelings. I knew that Veronica was a true friend and confidante who loved me and would support me no matter what. It was difficult, though, for me to overcome my insecurities enough to accept the love and friendship of her family. One incident during a holiday season helped me to overcome some of my insecurities. Veronica approached me in church before our pre-Thanksgiving service.

"Hi, Barbara. Were you still planning to go out to eat for Thanksgiving tomorrow?" she asked.

"Yes," I said. "Joey's parents are still out of town and Joey has to work part of the day. I don't feel like cooking this year. It really doesn't feel the same without Joey's parents and my mom around."

"Well, my mother called and told me to be sure to invite your family to have Thanksgiving with us. She didn't want you eating out in a restaurant when you should be with us like you used to be before you got married again," she said.

"Really? You have such a big family and there are six of us—"

"She knows that, but she really wants you all there," she said.

Before I could think about asking Joey if it was OK with him, I smiled with an enthusiastic, "Yes. I can't wait!"

I saw Veronica's cousin Karen in church and she also encouraged me to come to the family dinner. She told me that I was family and they enjoyed my visits. It hit me—just as it had hit Sally Fields at the Oscars when she said, "You like me, you really like me." I started crying right in church. I don't think anyone realized how important that seemingly small gesture was too me.

It was a wonderful Thanksgiving and a magnificent Christmas. We were invited to Dawn's new home for Christmas dinner and we received the same warm and loving welcome at her home that we received on Thanksgiving from Veronica's family. My children call my friends "Auntie Dawn" and "Auntie Veronica." They are truly my sisters in spirit. Dawn calls me her sister and mentioned how happy she was that her daughter Alena could play with her "cousins" on Christmas.

During the Kwanzaa season, the seven-day African-American cultural celebration that begins on December 26, Veronica's family celebrates each night at a different family member's home. On one particular night, one of Veronica's aunts said that next year I should host a night, as I was part of the family. I felt like I finally had my own nuclear family, wonderful in-laws, great friends, extended family, and a church family. My desire for family was finally being met. The only part that was still missing was my birth family.

PART IV
Finding My Roots

9

Seeking My Roots

Two thousand four would be a year of great healing. It would bring me great joy,
but also open up a lot of old wounds. In order to be healed, there is often a process of reflection and revisiting buried feelings.

In February, Joey and I took our first vacation together that didn't involve visiting family or friends. It also was our first time alone together that wasn't within
a few hours driving distance from the children. We decided to celebrate Valentine's Day in Miami. We both love Florida and Joey is especially fond of Miami
Beach. We left the cold temperatures of Massachusetts and headed south to the
warmth of Miami.

On our first night, we sat on a pier in Miami and just watched the beautiful
beach and the moon. The quiet was intoxicating. Most of the winter vacationers
were on the strip dancing or eating while we were getting some overdue relaxation. We enjoyed our time alone and the freedom to sleep in and go wherever
we wanted without worrying about the kids. He was able to do things he liked at
the swap meet, and I was able to visit the monkeys at Monkey Jungle, in between
taking in all of the local sights and beaches. It was our time to reconnect. Little
did I know I would be doing a lot of reconnecting in the following months.

There were many times before and after our trip that I would enter a deep-
thought state and feel as if I were having visions—like the character Raven on the
TV show *That's So Raven*. I would see things or people in my thoughts and soon

after I would actually run into them. People often get feelings of déjà vu and I figured that was what was happening to me, except that mine were more like premonitions. On one such day, one of my visions would have a great impact on the rest of my life.

I was stopped at a red light next to the local Christian bookstore. I was envisioning how several months earlier I bumped into my old friend Leslie's father. We caught up on our families' news. One of his sons was very ill and I told him I would pray for him. As I was recalling this past interaction, I began to think about another old friend, Karna. The last time I had an in-depth conversation with her was many years earlier when our kids swam on the Sharks swim team together, just as we did when we were their age. I was thinking about the things we had in common and the different paths that our lives had taken. We were both adopted and were both good students but our careers were very different. I became a nurse and she went into cosmetology. I also thought about how my first marriage failed, but hers did not. As the light was about to change, I thought, "That was weird thinking so long and hard about her."

When the light changed, I drove into a drug-store parking lot and went in to make a few purchases. As I walked down the store aisle still thinking about Karna, I bumped right into her! The whole thing was very strange. I told her how I'd just been thinking about her at the traffic light, and she also found our bumping into each other very strange. We began catching up on the important events in our lives. She told me that she and her husband were separating. I had just been thinking that I was such a failure for having divorced my first husband, while she was still married. I was able to give her some advice about how to deal with a separation or divorce as it relates to having small children. I also told her about my walk with the Lord. We had a reunion right there in the aisle at the drug store.

We also discussed our other common thread, adoption. She and her sister, who was also adopted, both started and stopped searches throughout the years, just as I had. They were also given a non-identifying informational letter that provided some details about their biological parents, just like the one I had been given. One of the things she discovered was that she inherited her birth mother's swimming skills. They were both excellent swimmers. This entire conversation, coupled with the strange thoughts I had prior to seeing Karna, reignited my fire to find my birth mother.

When I went home, I looked for the letter that included my non-identifying information. I had lost and found this letter many times. When I searched for it this time, it was missing again. Every time I read the one-page document, I would discover something I had forgotten since the last time I read it. This, along with the "Tanya" letter, would always become misplaced. It was as though I couldn't handle reading them and put them somewhere for safekeeping, but then forgot where I put them. I decided to call Child and Family Services the next day to get a copy of the letter, even though I wasn't sure that was the agency that had handled my adoption.

The only place I ever recalled my mom mentioning regarding my adoption was Brightside, and that was always done in moments of anger. She threatened to send me back to Brightside if I acted up. I realized later that she didn't mean what she said, but the words hurt just the same. Remembering these words reminded me that saying hurtful things was an area I knew I had to work on as well. I have made damaging remarks to others in anger that, despite whatever the provocation may have been, shouldn't have been said. It is written in *Proverbs* that words can be very detrimental. Even after an apology, the effects can last a lifetime.

The next day, I called Child and Family Services and spoke with a part-time counselor who sounded frail and elderly. She told me to send $70 with a written request for the non-identifying information, which I did promptly. I was very eager once again to have my hands on that letter. My stops and starts in my search were always like this. I would go full force, then get discouraged, or, it would bring up feelings I couldn't handle, and then I would stop. I was hoping that this time would be different. Since it would take several weeks for the letter to come, I decided, as I had done so many times before, to try other avenues. I was on a mission again. I obtained a list of phone numbers with my birth mother's name from the Internet white pages, but didn't have the nerve to make the calls. I thought that she probably didn't have the same name and was probably married with a family. I also wasn't entirely sure the name I had was correct. Maybe my mom read the name incorrectly. Maybe it was a pseudonym. Maybe it was a lie. Maybe, maybe, maybe. Maybe I was afraid that there was a lot I didn't know and a chance I would never find out.

I decided to log onto my old friend, "www.adoption.com." It had links to many related sites. As I surfed the web, I found a site that charged no money unless they found the person you were looking for or their next of kin. I decided to take a chance and immediately filled out the information form and sent it in. Within a few minutes I received a message that said, "Here is a copy of the quote we sent you last year, it is the same." There was a quote of nineteen hundred dollars, with a copy of the same information, as I'd sent it a year before. This was yet another example of my searching and then stopping and not even remembering what I had done. I had no recollection of filling out that form to Kinsolving Investigations or locating that site on the Internet. Some painful things are buried until we can handle them or something makes us remember them—just like when I suddenly remembered years later what Chrissy's brother tried to do to me when I was a little girl.

I printed the form, signed it, and faxed it to them immediately, without even reading it. In my excitement and haste I thought I was signing a request when in reality, it was a contract. I was tired of doing the searching myself. The work was much too painful for me. If it were meant to be, they would find her. If not, then I would stop searching for good. After sending it, I didn't give it another thought. I assumed it was a lost cause. If my birth mother wanted to find me, she would have already done so.

All of my life, it was my birth mother I'd been seeking—her and her children, if any. I longed for the details and circumstances of my birth as much as I longed for siblings. I wanted to know if she thought about me on my birthdays as my adoptive mom had assured me. My mom portrayed my birth mother as a caring and brave young woman who loved me. She said that there was no way a woman could carry a baby for nine months and not wonder about her through the years.

The day I faxed the form was a day at work like most others. Children came in for medications and for me to tend to their wounds and worries. It was a Friday afternoon. I was looking forward to my son John's birthday party the next week. At 3:30 PM, I received a cell-phone call from a Kinsolving Investigations representative.

The voice on the other end told me that they had found my birth mother. I couldn't believe what I was hearing. I had only faxed the form a few hours earlier. I was always told that if something seems too good to be true, it probably isn't true; and this was too good to be true. Anxiety, fear, doubts, and excitement were all traveling through my body at the same time. The voice said to send a certified check and they would send me the information. It was Friday afternoon—too late to do that. I had to agonize about it all weekend. If it had not been Friday I probably would have run straight to the bank without processing the information I'd been given.

I called Joey and Veronica right away. They were both as amazed as I was. They were both also a little skeptical. Veronica told me to check out the organization just to make sure they were legitimate. I also had some concerns. It was an Internet site. What if I sent the money and they sent me nothing? What if they were a fraud? My mom had taught me to make wise financial decisions and since her death I never wanted to waste any money, especially money she'd left to me. I thought that if I made an unwise financial decision, it would be disrespectful to her. I didn't know what to do. I decided to spend the weekend thinking and praying about it, hoping to have an answer by Monday morning. I picked up my children and told them the news. Of course, the little ones had no clue, but India and Brittany were very excited. They told me to just do it. We went out to eat to celebrate. Finally, the ball was in my hands.

I spent the next day looking over the contract, calling the Better Business Bureau, and praying. I also read a newsletter they published with comments from satisfied customers. I thought, "I bet those people are fake, anyone can make up a name and a letter and put it on a web site." After reading the contract carefully, I realized that all of the money was due when they successfully completed the search. All of this had my head spinning. I had to just keep praying.

The next day was Communion Sunday. I teach Children's Church every Sunday except the first Sunday of the month, when Children's Church is not in session. I always look forward to Communion Sunday and attending church with my family. As we were sitting together in church, a visitor took a seat next to me. She was a young, white woman with hazel eyes. My birth mother had been a young, white woman with hazel eyes. I shared my Bible and hymnal with her in an effort to show her Christian love and make her feel welcome. I chatted with her when I could. At the end of the service when there is a call for new members, I pushed my purse aside to make room for her to get up. I instinctively knew that she was going to join that day. She looked at me and said, "Is that how you join the church?" I responded an enthusiastic, "Yes!" She told me that she had been visiting for a while and felt that this was her day to join. Bonnie stepped out of the pew and walked up to the front of the church and joined St. John's that day.

This rare occurrence of a white woman with hazel eyes sitting next to me in a predominantly black church was the sign I was praying for. I decided right then and there that I would take the chance and send the money in the morning. Needless to say, once I made that decision, I was anxious for the rest of the day and didn't sleep a wink that night. This was what I had been dreaming about all my life.

I sent the certified check that Monday and then had to wait for the email to arrive the next day. I will never forget that day. It was March 2004 and it happened to be my youngest son, John's, birthday. I was trying to keep my mind off the email that was supposed to arrive soon, but I had a hard time focusing on anything. In between each student's visit to my office, I would check my email again.

The agency told me that they would send the email as soon as they received the certified check. They said that the mail usually came around 10 AM. By noontime, I was so anxious I couldn't sit still in my seat. I called the agency to see what was taking so long. They said the mail was late. Within a few minutes of my call to them, they called me back to say the check had arrived and the email was on its way. I logged on and waited for what I thought would be brief letter with the name of my birth mother and her contact information. What I found was even better. It not only had her contact information but it also contained pages and pages about her family's history, back to Europe.

It was more information than I cared about at the time. All I wanted to know was if the name of my birth mother, the one my adoptive mother had given me as a child, was correct, and if there was information about how to contact her. After receiving the email, I began to feel like I was the little "Tanya" again and my life was not just a great, big concocted lie. But what would I do with this information? Part of me always thought I would never know the answers to my questions. The other part of me imagined the upcoming phone call—the one that had been in my mind all my life.

I would say, "I was born in October 1963 and my given name was Tanya." She would cry and say she always wondered where I was, how I was doing, and that she always loved me. That was my fantasy. Now I had to face my reality.

I had to settle on how I would contact her. I could make the phone call. I could skip the phone call and show up at her house. I was excited, yet confused. I didn't know anyone who had found a birth parent, so I didn't know where to get advice. Finally, I called Chris at Kinsolving Investigations and voiced my concerns to her.

Chris told me that the first contact was the most important. I had to be prepared for the worst. My birth mother could deny that she knew anything about me or she could tell me to never contact her again. Despite my excitement, I again had to face all of my lifelong fears of rejection. Chris told me that I should wait at least a day so that I could prepare myself emotionally for the first contact. She suggested writing a letter. I rejected that idea. I thought that she could get the letter and move or change her number without ever hearing my voice. I knew I wanted to make the phone call. Chris suggested that I not shock her with the words that I had rehearsed in my mind for so many years. She gave me some suggestions about how to break the news more slowly and said that I could call her back if I needed more guidance. I thanked her for finding my birth mother and for the emotional support and guidance. I took her advice but couldn't wait until the next day.

I shared my good news with Veronica and Dawn. They were both overjoyed. At first, Dawn thought that when I said I had good news, it was that I was pregnant. When I told her that I had contact information for my birth mother, she was overwhelmed to the point of tears. She wanted to know my plans for contacting her and told me to tell my birth mother that I had a younger sister named Dawn. Joey was also very supportive and excited, as was Veronica.

Usually when I get home from work our house is filled with the noise of television, radio, cooking in the kitchen, and my boys running to the door to greet me to tell me how their day was. On this day, however, the house was deathly quiet and still. Joey picked up the children and no one was home yet. I was a little disappointed because I wanted to share my news with everyone. In the midst of the tranquility, it occurred to me that Chris suggested that I make the first call when I was alone and in a quiet place. I decided that it was time to make the call. I went upstairs to my bedroom and locked the door. I had butterflies in my stomach. I was so nervous I could barely dial the number. I sat on my bed, picked up the phone, and made the call I had dreamed about making all my life.

I had a list of questions prepared, as Chris recommended, just in case this would be our only conversation. As the phone rang, I became more and more uneasy. Finally, a woman answered the phone.

"May I please speak with Joanne White?" came out of my mouth.

"This is Joanne."

My heart was racing so fast I could barely breathe.

"Hi, my name is Barbara Gowan and I would like to talk with you for a few minutes about a personal matter. Do you have a moment to talk?"

"Yes," she said.

"I was born in October 1963 and named Tanya Elizabeth. Is this still a good time to talk?"

She said "yes" but that she wanted to change phones so she could converse out on her porch. She said that she had just got a computer and had been planning to try to find me. That was music to my ears. I told her that I didn't want to write a letter, as I was afraid someone would find it and that could cause her problems if no one knew about me. Of course that was only one of my reasons.

I asked, "Do you mind if I ask you a few questions?'

She said, "OK."

So far, so good, I thought.

I continued, "Are you married, and do you have any other children?"

"Yes, I am married. My husband and I are like best friends. I also have a son and a daughter."

"Does anyone know about me?" I asked.

"My husband and my daughter know about you, but they don't know you are black."

That didn't surprise me.

"I told my daughter about you when she was pregnant and I told my husband about you a long time ago," she continued.

I interrupted and said, "I just want you to know that I always had positive feelings about you. My mother told me that you must have been a brave and loving woman to carry me for nine months then give me to a family that could care for me. She also told me that you may not have been given a choice about keeping me or not and that times were much different back then."

"I wasn't given a choice. Times were much different then. Someone from the college called my parents and told them I was pregnant. They came and picked me up and told me I had to give you up for adoption. I was sent to live with relatives in Massachusetts until you were born. They said it was the best thing for everyone."

"Was it because you were pregnant by a black man?" I asked.

"No. It was just because I was only nineteen and unmarried," she replied.

She had questions of her own. She began with "Did you have good parents?"

"Yes I had good parents. I actually looked like I belonged to them. My mom was very light and my dad was darker in complexion. I fit right in."

"I told the adoption agency that I wanted you to be raised in a black family," she added.

I wondered why she wanted me raised in a black family and why that even crossed her mind, but I never asked her.

"What do you look like?" she asked.

"I have light skin and dark, curly hair. I have an athletic shape with a small waist and big hips. I also have a cleft in my chin. I always wondered where I got my traits.

"What do you look like?" I asked next.

"When I was younger, I was very pretty. I have big hips, so does my daughter. I also have a similar cleft in my chin. You can see it in one of my baby photos."

I didn't tell her but I had always assumed I got my hips from the black side of my family.

"Do you have any children?" she asked.

"Yes, I have four kids, two girls and two boys"

"Where are you living?"

"I live in Springfield, Massachusetts."

She said, "You still live there?" And then, "They changed your name?"

I guess she thought I would always be called Tanya.

She said, "I lived near Riverside Amusement Park when I was pregnant with you. I used to take long walks near the park that summer."

"I take my kids there all the time," I said. "Now it is called Six Flags Amusement Park, but I remember when it was called Riverside. I went there when I was a young child."

I thought it was strange that I probably drove right past the house she lived in many times on my way to that park.

"Was your family very supportive to you when you were pregnant?" I asked.

"No. I actually was alone for your birth."

That made me sad just thinking about her alone like that.

"Did you hold me after I was born?"

"Yes, but they only let me hold you for one minute. Then they took you away."

I felt sad for her, and then I felt sad for myself. We both lost the connection that we had for nine months in that instant.

I was so anxious during our conversation that I was afraid that I wouldn't retain all of the information that she was giving me, so I decided to start writing it down.

"Do you remember what hospital I was born in?" I asked.

"No. I only remember that you were adopted through a Catholic agency."

"Do you remember the time I was born, or my length or weight?" These were things I always wanted to know.

"No, I only remember it was in the morning and I was in a lot of pain."

I then figured I might never know the answers to those questions; but I still had more to ask.

"Are you Italian?"

"No, I am English and Irish. Why did you think I was Italian?" she asked.

"I was mistaken for Italian when I was younger, so I thought you might have been Italian. Did you go back to college after I was born?"

"No, and I was very smart. I graduated first in my class."

"Wow. I graduated first in my class also."

"I worked for a long time until I got diagnosed with lung cancer. I used to smoke a lot. I shed a lot of tears worrying that I would die and not know what happened to you."

She probably had no idea how important it was to me to know she thought about me and always wondered what happened to me.

"Do you still have cancer?" I asked.

"No. I stopped smoking after I was diagnosed. I finished all of my treatments, and now I am cancer-free. I do have other health problems though. I have arthritis, varicose veins, and stomach problems."

The sketchy details of my medical history on my adoption papers were now being filled in. Just as I thought, there was more to it than "no hereditary diseases that we know of." Those words never made much sense to me, as most young mothers haven't been alive long enough to know what they could be passing down to their children. I told her that I also had varicose veins in one leg despite my love of exercise and being in good shape and that I, too, had problems with my stomach. I was happy to hear that after chemotherapy and radiation treatments she was free from cancer.

We traded a few more commonalities in our lives. We both had suffered the loss of parents. Both of my parents were deceased and she had recently lost her mother. We also were both cheerleaders. I thought these similarities were amazing. After that, she asked if she could call me back because her husband was home and she didn't feel comfortable talking any longer. Panic crept into my body. Chris warned me that this could be a sign that the contact would end.

I asked, "Can I call you back another time if you can't call me later?"

She said, "Yes." She then reassured me that she would call me back when I returned from church that evening.

Before hanging up, I was compelled to ask about my birth father in case this would prove to be our only conversation.

"One last thing." I paused. "Can you tell me what my birth father's name is?"

"Yes. It is James Leflore."

"How long were you two together?"

"Briefly."

"Was he a nice man?"

"Yes, he was a very nice man," she said before saying goodbye.

I was inundated with information. My head was spinning. I was ecstatic beyond words. If I never heard from her again, at least I finally heard some of the words that I needed to hear to fulfill the "marrow-deep hunger," and "hollow yearning" described in Alex Haley's writings.

I had to have faith that she would indeed call back, and she did so, many more times. When she called back after I returned from church, she told me more about her son and daughter. She said that they were very close. In fact, her daughter lived in the same apartment complex she lived in. She told me that after our first conversation, she called her daughter to tell her all about my finding her.

She gave me her daughter's email address and phone number and said I could send photos to her there. She told me again that she and her husband were like best friends and even though she had told him about me years ago, she wasn't ready to tell him that I had contacted her. I completely understood.

I tried to send photos to her daughter's email address, but my computer kept freezing. I called her daughter, Angie's, house to let her know that I was unable to send the photos but I would try the next day. She told me that when her mom called to tell her about me, she'd been crying "happy tears." That made my night complete.

As much as I wanted to share my news, there was a part of me that first night that wanted to lie in bed and just think about all I had experienced that day. I was emotionally drained. The next day I was on top of the world and I shared my good news with my friends. Everyone was very happy for me. I was happy for myself; and it kept getting better. That morning, I received an email from my half-sister, Angie:

Barbara, Hi. How are you? This is Angie your half sister I guess. Wow! I received your emails but I don't want to view them before my mom, as I know she is anxious to see you. I called her this morning and she had just gotten to sleep at around 8 am so she will be coming by later. I just think I should let her see you and read your email first. I hope you don't think that is weird. But I knew you would want to see some pictures, so I have attached a few. I don't have too many pictures on my computer except tons of my baby. But my mom has some pictures that she is bringing over today to send to you. I hope that you are not too disappointed that I have not sent more … I can't wait to see your pictures and I know my mom is very excited … bye for now … talk to you soon.

Angie

I was so excited to see photos of my birth mother for the first time. I received pictures of the whole family including a photo of my mother when she was four months pregnant with me. I could see a resemblance in photos from her college years. She had the same cleft in her chin and similarly shaped eyes and cheeks. What was more amazing was that Angie and I looked alike. She wore her hair like mine and looked rather "Italian" like I did when I was younger. It was probably because she was part Greek. Another milestone was reached. I finally saw someone who looked like me, besides my children. The emails kept coming:

Hi Barbara, My mom just left and wanted me to send you an email. She may send one herself or talk to you if you call her tonight … we both agree that you are very beautiful. I do see some of me and my mom in you. I know with the pictures it is so hard to tell. Mom has this one picture of her years ago hanging on her wall where her hair is black and straight and long. She forgot to bring it over but I will send it tomorrow. Thank you so much for the compliment about me that was very sweet. But you made me laugh when you said we were built differently. All throughout school I was referred to as having a booty meant for a black girl. I hope that that doesn't offend you, it never offended me … My mom said you were a cheerleader, so was I. My mom talked to my dad last night and it turns out that when she told him of you years ago, she already mentioned that you were biracial so all that worry for nothing. My dad was only worried that maybe I would be hurt. But I am OK. This is a lot to take in but not nearly as much as you. I just wish it wouldn't be so hard to find people. I would never have dreamed in a million years my mom would be that hard to find. It makes me sad. Your family is beautiful. We enjoyed the pictures … we would love to see pictures of you growing up. I must tell you my mom was overcome with emotions when she saw your picture. You really are a very, very beautiful woman. Bye for now. Take care!!

Angie

My mother emailed me later saying, "I am so happy that you found me! We will meet someday!" She also told me that she loved me.

When I first contacted my birth mother, she was ill. She told me that she didn't want to meet me until she felt better. I prayed and prayed for her health to return. About a month later, she told me that she had tests run and stopped taking her medication and the doctor said it seemed to be a miracle; she had just got better with no explanation. I thought to myself, "Prayer works!" She was happy to be able to crochet and enjoy her meals again. She seemed very upbeat.

She talked about her upcoming summer vacation with joy. She was going to see her son who was expecting a baby. Since he lived only a few hours away from me, I asked if I could meet her somewhere. She didn't think it was a good idea. When she said that, I felt like I wanted to die. I thought she would be excited that I would travel to see her, even if for just a few minutes. I wasn't looking to meet the whole family; I just wanted to finally see her in person. I wanted to touch the woman who gave me life and give her a hug. I realized at that point, she didn't feel the same. She could sense the disappointment in my voice. She explained that she hadn't told her husband about all of our phone calls, and she hadn't told her son about me at all. She said she didn't want to feel like she was sneaking off to meet me. I understood, but it hurt just the same.

Joanne was also concerned about how her daughter and husband would be affected by my finding her. This was the first time I actually began to cry. I am usually very emotional and was amazed I didn't cry sooner, even happy tears—through all of this news. I began to feel very protective toward her, just like I was for my adoptive mom. I didn't want to cause her any pain or grief. It truly saddened me to think that my presence was causing anyone anything but joy. This was the catalyst that opened the door to the floodgate of my pent-up emotions. I cried and cried and cried. I am sure some of the tears were happy tears, some sad tears, and some just from being overwhelmed at the enormity of the whole situation. A lot had happened over a short period.

Angie wrote me again the next day reassuring me that I hadn't caused anyone any grief. She said she could tell I was a very emotional person, just like she and her mom were. She said she used to watch adoption reunion stories on TV and wonder what it would be like if her mom ever found me. She said that she and her mom are very sensitive and get hurt easily; that was the reason for her dad's concern. I began to think that the strong emotions and sensitivity were genetic.

She thought I was a strong woman. She said, "You are sitting there worrying about us and I sit here happy for you. I can't imagine or begin to imagine what this is all like for you. So if deep down somewhere I have any insecurity about all of this, it is certainly outweighed by shear joy when I think of you and how happy and excited you sound. So please don't worry about me, I am OK." Her words helped a lot at the time. I was grateful for all of the kindness she had shown me and felt fulfilled beyond my wildest dreams. I was also excited because I had the name of my birth father.

10

The Black Side

o o o o o o o o o o o o o o o o o o o o o o o o o o o o o o o o o o o o
Blood ties are what makes us from the same family, but shared life experiences is what makes a family.

—*From "The Search Guru"—Colleen Bruckner*

During most of my life, I never thought about finding my birth father. I always had the impression that many men have "outside" children who are a secret, and they don't want to be involved with them. I always figured it would be that way with my birth father, too. Shortly before searching for my birth mother, my thoughts on this matter changed. I heard about the movie *Antwone Fisher*. In it, a boy in foster care is abused. The main reason I wanted to watch it was because Denzel Washington was directing and starring in it.

Brittany and I settled down comfortably in my bed to watch the movie one night. I was mentally prepared for the scenes of abuse that I knew were depicted in the story. After all, I came in contact with social problems on a daily basis on my job. I thought I had built up a solid emotional wall. I was not, however, prepared for the poignant scene near the end of the movie. At the urging of his mentor, Antwone decided to find his biological family in order to continue his journey toward healing his childhood issues. Within a few days, he had contacted his deceased father's sister. She was eager to meet him. He also met an uncle who knew where his birth mother lived and took Antwone to meet her.

I was totally traumatized by her reaction when she met her son. I thought that she could not have been more cold, distant, or detached. Antwone told his mother that he was a good man. He stayed away from drugs and hadn't fathered any children out of wedlock. He let her know that he had done well in spite of his circumstances. She said very little and didn't even want to hug him. I thought that he must have felt like dying inside. I began to sob uncontrollably. There was nothing I could do to stop the flood of tears or the sickening feeling in the pit of my stomach.

In the next scene, Antwone returned to his aunt's home. There were a multitude of relatives waiting there to welcome him into the family. They doted on this young man who looked very much like his father. They showed him the love and acceptance that was lacking in the meeting with his mother. Brittany couldn't understand my tears. I tried to explain to her that I hoped someday someone in my birth family would be that happy to meet me. I experienced an epiphany: I realized it was just as important to find my father, as it was to find my mother!

At first I thought about paying the same agency that found my birth mother to find my birth father, but then I decided to try on my own first. I called Syracuse University and asked if they had any information on a James Leflore who was a student there in the early 1960s.

I was told that they had that information, but were not at liberty to give it to me. She offered to email him and give him my contact information, but I was too impatient for that.

I procured a list of all the James Leflores in the United States. There weren't very many, so I thought it might not be too difficult to find him. I began with the ones in New York. The very first call met with success. A woman answered the phone and when I asked if this was the home of a James Leflore from Syracuse University, she said, "Yes it is," and then called out, "Jim, you have a phone call." Once again, my spur-of-the-moment actions had me reeling with all kinds of emotions. I was nervous and anxious, and he got to the phone before I could figure out what to say.

I was so unprepared that I am sure I jumbled my words. I asked if he remembered a girl by the name of Joanne White from Syracuse University. He said the name wasn't familiar, but that it was a long time ago. I just assumed he would say "yes" and then I could explain who I was. This was harder, his not remembering. I told him my name and that I had recently located my birth mother and she gave me the name James Leflore as my birth father. There was dead silence on the other end of the phone. I broke the silence by launching into a series of questions:

"Are you a tall, light-skinned man?" I asked.

"Yes."

"Were you from upstate New York?"

"Yes."

"Were you studying to be a doctor?"

"Yes. I have a Ph.D. in anthropology."

Finally, I asked him about the last thing Joanne mentioned to me about him. "Were you seeing a white woman other than my mother in college?"

"Yes. I married her before entering the military," was his final answer to my litany of questions.

I seemed to have the right person. I told him that I had a good life and only wanted to know about my roots. I wanted nothing else. He asked a few questions about me. I told him that I was a school nurse and was married with four children and a stepdaughter. I offered to email him a photo of me. Then, he paused. The reality of the situation was hitting him. I realized I had caught him off guard and asked if he wanted me to call him back in a few days. He said "yes." I later wondered why he asked me so many questions about myself if he hadn't remembered my birth mother. Maybe he was just curious.

I was overwhelmed and flabbergasted at the fact that after stopping and starting several searches for many years, I now had talked to my birth mother and birth father within two days of getting the email from the investigators and five days after returning the search form. All this had stemmed from those visions about Karna and my subsequent chance meeting with her. I may have waited another few years to get up the nerve to search again if not for the strange events of that day. I was overjoyed by the fact that my search was now over. I was also thrilled that every time I turned on the computer there was a new email from my half-sister, whom I got to know very well.

I called James Leflore back in a few days. It was Saturday. I thought all morning about what I would say. I didn't know what time to call, so I decided to wait until at least noon. I was nervous all morning. I had a good feeling that he would remember who my birth mother was. I thought maybe I just caught him off guard when we first spoke. Even if he did remember her when I first called, he still would have to process all that I told him. It had been three days. I would find out if he knew her and could be my birth father, or didn't know her, or just didn't want to explore the possibility. Either way, I had to know. I went up to my bedroom and closed the door, then sat on my bed and dialed, just as I had when I called Joanne. The phone rang. Someone picked up and it sounded like the very distinguished man I spoke with a few days earlier.

"Hi. May I please speak with James LeFlore?"

"Hi. Is this Barbara?" he asked.

"Yes," I said.

Before I could say anything else he interrupted—

"I was afraid you wouldn't call back. I remembered who Joanne was after we hung up the phone and I realized you never gave me your phone number. I am so glad you called back."

"I wanted to call back sooner, but I thought I would give you some time," I said.

"The reason I didn't remember her name at first was because I knew her by Jo, not Joanne, and I was caught off-guard when you called."

"I'm sorry I caught you off guard. You were the first person I called and was actually surprised and caught off guard when you got on the phone. I never called looking for my birth father before and didn't really know the right thing to say myself. So, you do remember Joanne, right?"

"Yes. We spent a brief time together."

"So, do you think you could be my birth father?" I asked

"Well, the dates do line up and I was with her during that time. I can't imagine she would say I was your father if it weren't so," he responded.

"Did you know about me?" I asked.

"I didn't know what happened to Joanne," he said. "She was in college and then all of the sudden she was gone. I didn't know where she went or what happened with her."

"Oh." I didn't know what to say. That wasn't how I had imagined their relationship. In my childhood fantasy, they were in love and he was involved and supportive and wanted to keep me but couldn't because their families wouldn't allow it. At least I was finally learning the real story.

"There was a lot going on at that time. I was drafted into the military, got married, and then relocated out of New York all in a short period of time," he said.

"Did you have to go to Vietnam?" I asked, knowing it was during that era that many young men had to go overseas to fight.

"No, I didn't have to go to Vietnam. I had a college education so they were able to use my skills in areas other than combat."

I was happy to hear that. If he had to fight in Vietnam, he may have been killed and I wouldn't have been able to find him.

"Are you still married?" I asked.

"Yes, but not to the woman I married when I was drafted."

I wasn't happy to know he'd been divorced, but I did think that if he were married to the same woman and I was conceived prior to their marriage, she might not be happy about me popping up now.

"That was my wife who answered the phone when you called the other day. It was a coincidence that you actually reached me at home when you called. We both work at the university and we had just finished eating lunch and were on our way back to work. If you had called a few minutes later, no one would have been home," he said.

It wasn't a coincidence, I thought to myself. It was God's perfect timing.

"I work at a school and have also taught, but not at a university," I replied.

I was interested in his career and what he taught, but I changed the subject, as I was really interested to know if I had any siblings.

"Do you have any children?" I asked.

"Yes. A son and a daughter."

"Wow. My birth mother also has a son and a daughter. How old are yours?"

"Randy is 40 and Michelle is—

Before he could finish I said, "I am also 40." I realized that his son and I were less than a year apart. I learned that he married their mother after he was drafted. He'd been in a serious relationship with their mom, and dated my birth mother when they were briefly estranged. He and his wife reunited and started their own family after I was conceived. That wasn't how I imagined it, but at least now I knew the truth.

"Can you tell me about my sister?"

"She is very smart like you. She is an engineer. Randy is in the restaurant business."

He went on to tell me about each of them and to tell me about his very large family that included a brother who was a plastic surgeon, a brother who was an attorney in Manhattan, a brother who was a businessman, and another brother and sister who were educators. He explained he also had two half-sisters. I was excited to hear all about his very large family. I wanted to know more about all of them but decided to change the subject to one that had always caused me much concern—my medical history.

Most people take that information for granted, but as an adoptee you are reminded of that missing piece of the puzzle of your life every time you see a new physician and are asked about your family history. I hated having to respond, "I don't know, I was adopted." The physician then leaves all of those important spaces on your history blank—just another reminder of the many missing pieces of my life that I may have never been able to fill in. He informed me about the medical problems in the LeFlore family and I wrote it all down. No one wants to find out that they may be at risk for hereditary medical problems, but I was happy to finally find out and excited about going to my next physical and being able to fill in the missing pieces on my history.

I then began wondering what he looked like. I asked him if he wanted me to send him some photos of myself on line and he said yes. I then asked him if he could send me some as well. He said that he could but that if I wanted to see what he looked like sooner rather than later, I could visit his University web site. He gave me the web address and I couldn't wait to take a look.

My father was talkative like me. He was also a good student. I was impressed as he explained his professional career. He said he was also impressed by my academic and professional accomplishments. I told him that my photograph had been in the newspaper several times and he said he wanted to see them all. I told him I would send him some of the newspaper articles written about me. I sent him photos in the paper from when I was class Valedictorian, a photo ad I did to promote Baystate Medical Center, an article that ran front page in the newspaper about my life as a visiting nurse, as well as a brochure from Rutgers that featured my photograph. He also asked for some of my personal family photos.

As much as I enjoyed talking with him, I was once again emotionally drained. I was talking and writing at the same time and my head was spinning from all I was hearing. I told him I wanted to go to his Web site to match the voice with a face and he said he looked forward to doing the same when I e-mailed him my photos.

As soon as I hung up I went to his web site. He was handsome and had an impressive career. I could now connect the voice on the phone with a face; one that my family said was very similar to mine. He emailed me later that day saying that it was a shock to learn about a daughter he never knew he had. He was glad that I made the effort to connect and wanted to develop a relationship. He said that I sounded like the type of person who would make any father proud. Over the next week, we talked and emailed and shared photos and histories. He sent me a photograph taken when he was in college. I now had photographs of both of my biological parents around the time they were together. I could replace the story and picture I had created in my mind with the facts. None of this was how I had imagined. It was better, because it was real.

At this point, I had to come to terms with a lot of emotions. I knew that if there were ever a time that I needed therapy, it was now. I met with a counselor who helped me deal with the unresolved feelings I was experiencing about being adopted and about finally connecting with my biological parents. I needed help trying to understand not only my own feelings but also what my biological parents were going through in order to know best how to proceed in our new relationships.

For Joanne, I was no longer an unwanted pregnancy that had been taken care of. I was a biracial woman with a name and a face and feelings. She also had to deal with how this might affect her children and her husband. More important, she had to face whatever unresolved feelings she had about me. During one of our phone conversations she told me that she loved me. Loving me, yet knowing she had to let me go must have been difficult. My therapist said that my birth mother was probably experiencing shame and guilt, among many other emotions. I tried to reassure her that I had a good life and that I understood that she did what she had to do at the time. Those words probably didn't heal her wounds. I, too, had a lot of wounds to heal as I tried to deal with my feelings for her, and my feelings for my birth father.

Jim, as I began to call him, had a son and a daughter, and many siblings to take into consideration. He told me that he spoke with his younger sister Loretta a few days after our first phone call and told her all about me. He'd sent me a photo of her and said he knew I would love her. He thought I looked like Loretta. He said that he would tell his family members gradually and things would evolve, as they should, over time. I was especially excited whenever I thought about meeting my siblings. Patience isn't one of my virtues, but it was one I had to develop.

After I located both of my biological parents, I got a call back from Child and Family Services to tell me that the letter with my non-identifying information was complete for me to pick up. I thought about not picking it up since I had already found my birth mother and birth father, but finally decided to get it for my records. I told the woman who'd compiled the information for the letter I was about to receive that since first contacting her, I had found my biological parents.

I told her their names and she said, "You are correct."

She asked, "Did your father ever become a doctor?"

I don't know why, but that question made me angry. I am sure she meant no harm, but I felt violated. She held in her lap a thick file with the information I had been seeking all my life. She knew more about my birth than I did.

She was free to read things about me, and my biological parents, that I couldn't. It seemed so unfair. I had a deep yearning to know more. I wanted to know the time of my birth and my weight and height, for example, since Joanne couldn't remember any of that information. She looked through pages of medical files but couldn't find it. I wanted to read my own file. It was about me, but I knew I couldn't see it because the records are sealed. This was another reminder of the pieces of my life that I was denied, just like the first ten months of my life. A two-page letter was all I had to sum up most of my first year. People who are not adopted take for granted the information about their births and their firsts—first time walking, talking, smiling, laughing, etc. Many adopted children will have gaps in their lives that will remain unsolved mysteries. This woman was as helpful as she could be. I thanked her for the letter and put it in a safe place where it wouldn't be lost again.

I continued to develop relationships with both sides of my birth family. I also learned that everyone was not willing to receive me into my father's family with open arms. Some of his siblings were not sharing his joy. I got the feeling that everyone was not convinced that he was really my birth father. We had a lot in common, but aside from the similarities in appearance between Loretta and me, and Joanne's story, there was nothing that linked us. Some family members suggested that we get a blood test. I was happy with the idea because then I would know for sure. On the other hand, I was nervous because there was a chance I could find out that he wasn't my father. I had grown extremely attached to him and if he wasn't the right person, I might never find my actual birth father.

The morning after the blood test was suggested, a strange feeling came over me. The pain regarding the circumstances of my birth hit me. My mother once told me that she was ashamed because she was a bastard. I thought that was silly because there were so many children born out of wedlock that there was no longer a stigma attached to it. I never thought of myself as a bastard. I was adopted, but raised by a married couple. For all outward appearances, I was a child born of their marriage, loved and wanted in every sense, and that was how I'd always seen myself. When the suggestion of getting a blood test arose, it hit me—I was a bastard, too! I was conceived out of wedlock and my mother was not willing and/or able to take care of me. I finally understood the pain that my birth mother felt. The pent-up emotions erupted and I cried uncontrollably once again.

Jim didn't doubt that he was my biological father. The dates of his brief encounter with Joanne and my birth were in sync. The test, he said, was to remove doubt from everyone else's minds. He wanted to take care of me just like he did his other two children and the test would verify his paternity. It all sounded so logical. But emotions aren't controlled by logic. He said that if the blood tests proved that I wasn't his biological daughter, he still wanted to meet me because I was a wonderful person. However, he believed that the results would be what we both wanted.

In the meantime, we continued to get acquainted. I remember when I first sent him photos I had decided to send them in chronological order, because when I sent photos to Joanne I had started with recent photos but she then asked for pictures of me as a baby. I imagine that was because she remembered me as a baby. I thought he would want to see them also. When I first sent Jim photos, my computer froze after the first few went through. He called and said that the toddler and young child photos were nice, but he really wanted to see what I looked like now. I thought that was funny and realized they had different points of reference as to how I entered their lives. I did eventually work my way up to recent photographs and sent the copies of the newspaper articles, ads, and Rutgers brochure to him. As time went on, I sent him, as well as Joanne, a compilation of my home videos so that I could share with him all of the most important events in my life. Jim's wife, Cindy, said she saw a resemblance in our noses and eyebrows. When Jim saw the home movies, he said that he was happy to see that Joey seemed so devoted to me. He said that a father looks for those qualities in a son-in-law. He was also pleased that I had a supportive network of friends and family. On April 2, 2004, I received the letter confirming that Jim was my father. We were both elated and we made plans for him to come to visit me at the end of his teaching semester.

Two of Jim's sisters, Loretta and Pat, called me a few weeks later. I was beginning to feel like part of the family. I enjoyed talking to them and to my father. He was very protective of Joanne and cautioned me to take things slow with her. His theory was that it was a lot easier for him to develop a relationship with me because he had been unaware that I existed and was not burdened with the shame and guilt that she might have carried for years.

After both of my biological parents got to know me, each thought I was "pretty religious." I never thought of myself that way, but I can see how they might. I wanted more than anything to please God. I prayed for them consistently. Before talking with Loretta and Pat, Cindy seemed to be the only one who wanted to discuss my faith. She was happy that I was praying for her. There was a part of me that didn't want to discuss my faith with them because I know that religion can turn people off if they don't share the same views.

This hesitancy about talking about my faith made me uncomfortable because I knew it was based on some of my old insecurities and fears about not being accepted for the "real me." With the love of my friends and church family, I began to overcome those feelings. I had to accept the fact that they would either love or reject the "real me." I didn't want to pretend to be someone I was not. I was being tested about hiding a very important part of myself, my faith. I realized that I just had to let those fears go.

Mother's Day weekend was quickly approaching. It was hard to believe that so much had happened so quickly. My birth father was excited about coming to Massachusetts to meet me. We talked on the phone and sent emails frequently. I felt as if I had known him and Cindy for years. I shared things with him that would normally take years for me to tell anyone else. I thought, "What if he doesn't like me when he meets me?" Evidently, he was having similar thoughts that maybe I wouldn't like him either. He said that we were family now and we were stuck with each other. That statement gave me the same comforting feeling that I had when Joey told me that John would be ours and he would love him the same whether he was born with any health problems or not.

We talked about what I would feel comfortable calling him. I called my father-in-law "Dad" and couldn't imagine loving anyone else the way I loved him or my adoptive father. I told my new aunt Loretta that I couldn't wait until all of the newness was gone and we could relax and enjoy each other. It happened a lot sooner than I imagined.

While I was getting to know Jim and his family, our church was participating in a seven-week period of fasting and praying. During our daily prayer services, I shared my joy, enthusiasm, and anxiety with my church family about my birth father's impending first visit. They were more supportive than I could ever imagine. One of the new ministers, Angela, told me that sharing testimonies about trials and blessings is important, as it can be a source of encouragement for others. I thought my purpose was to be a great wife and mother, a great nurse and friend, while being a faithful Christian. I never thought my journey could be an inspiration to others.

I got more and more nervous as the reunion date in May 2004 approached. I took Friday off, knowing I was too anxious to concentrate on work. I spent the day cleaning places in my home I had never even noticed before. I must have tried on a dozen outfits before I settled on a simple white top to match the black and white skirt I had just purchased. I didn't like the way my hair looked so I asked my hairdresser, Carmen, to squeeze me in to do my hair again, even though I had just had it done the day before. I got a manicure and a pedicure, too. I wanted to look perfect.

Joey and I went to noontime prayer and announced that it was my big day. They prayed for me to have peace. Joey's mom volunteered to cook dinner for us that night, as she knew I would be too nervous to cook. Besides, she is one of the best cooks I know.

All of the kids were waiting patiently in the living room looking out of our picture window for their new grandfather. They called Joey's father "Papa Jay" so we decided they would call my father "Papa Jim." JJ and John, then ages seven and six respectively, didn't fully understand how they could be meeting a grandfather for the first time after all these years. I tried to explain to them that the woman who gave birth to me was young and couldn't take care of me, so she gave me to Nana Miller since Nana Miller couldn't have babies of her own. JJ seemed to get it but couldn't understand why the young woman couldn't take care of me. John just went along with the program.

Jim didn't want me to give him directions to my house. He wanted to find my home then just drive up and ring the doorbell. We got worried when he didn't arrive right on time. I tried to be patient by admiring the flowers we recently planted. He mentioned that he grew dahlias so I planted some of them in the back yard. Whenever I got relaxed, the kids would yell, "Here he is!" and then say, "psyche" and start laughing. They were driving me crazy. They yelled it once again, but this time I saw India and Brittany running out into the front yard. He was here at last!

I was so nervous I could barely breathe. He was standing in my front yard, smiling and holding a bouquet of roses. I didn't know what to do or say. Joey told me to run out and say "Hi, Dad!" But I couldn't do that. It all seemed so unnatural. I walked up to him. We hugged and took a good look at each other. While I put the roses in a vase, he went out to the car to get another gift. It was a beautiful wall clock that chimes every hour. I thought it signified the time we missed together. Because I didn't know what else to do, we went into the back yard to show him my dahlias and take the pictures that I had waited a lifetime to take.

We sat in the living room and talked. I was uncomfortable at first, watching him watching me. I tried not to stare at him but I wanted to take it all in. Just as I was thinking how glad I was that Joey and the kids were there, Joey suggested taking the kids to his mother's while we got to know each other. That caught me totally off guard. I became even more anxious. But as the evening went on, the nervousness subsided and we got better acquainted. I showed him the many photographs in my house. He commented about the number of pictures in my home. I told him that I was a "picture person" and I loved to collect frames.

As he looked at the silver frame with my adoptive mother's photo, he said, "She was very pretty."

I smiled and said, "That is my favorite picture of her." We spent a lot of time talking about her and my childhood. I then told him about how I started scrapbooking. After I'd received all of the photos of Joanne and her family, I was invited to a scrapbooking party. I took pride in doing my first page with my birth mother's photos. After I did that page, which was to be the first page of the scrapbook, I felt guilty and decided to start a scrapbook of not just my birth family but also my adoptive family and myself as well, to chronicle all of the important people in my life. I remember feeling uncomfortable when the people at the scrapbooking party said, "Oh, you are doing a scrapbook of your real mother?" and I felt as though I had to defend my adoptive mother and say, "No. I see my adoptive mother as my 'real mother.'"

The whole concept of who your "real mother" or "real father" is, is one that many of us in the adoptive community are uncomfortable with. It minimizes the significance of our adoptive families. I had no problem talking about everyone in my life with my birth father—except, that is, when I was showing him photos and talking about my adoptive dad, Harold. It is very strange saying "my dad" was like this or that when Jim was also my father. It was great, however, that he was very open and talkative and had a very sensitive side so that I could express all of my feelings, including the uncomfortable ones, with him. He was very understanding and supportive, as was Cindy.

The scrapbook was a very helpful way of guiding our conversations. Whenever I turned a page, I remembered stories from that era in my life, involving the people we were looking at. This gave them a picture to go with the story and a clearer view of my life before I met them. I was happy to tell them about my godmother Claire and many of my mother's friends whom I called "Auntie." Jim was happy to tell me about his sisters that I now could also call "Auntie." It was very emotional for me to talk about the many people who affected my life, especially Michelle. As we shared stories about ourselves, I felt more and more comfortable with them and more relaxed.

As I became more relaxed, I began sharing with them just how important it was for me to find them and feel a part of their family. Despite being loved and cared for by my adoptive family and my friends, I tried to explain how empty not knowing about my roots made me feel. It is one of those situations—like losing a loved one—where people around you say they understand or try to understand, but until it happens to them, they cannot truly grasp the significance of the event. I recall my father saying things like, "Well you had a good home, and now you have us," as though it were simple. For me, it wasn't that simple. I tried to articulate how being adopted affected so many areas of my life and that being adopted as well as knowing I was biracial seemed quite often to rule my emotions and the many important decisions I'd made in my life.

By the time we finished looking at the scrapbook and I had shared my feelings about being adopted, we were famished. We decided it was time to meet Joey and the kids at his parents' house. Joey's mother cooked all of our favorite, delicious, soul-food dishes. Jim said he hadn't had a meal like that in a long time. Veronica and her boyfriend Mike joined us for dinner. We talked until almost midnight. I was exhausted mentally and physically by the time Jim and Cindy left to go to the Marriot and we drove home and finally got to bed. It was one of the best nights I could remember and I had a wonderfully peaceful night's sleep. The worry and anxiety was over. Everything worked out fine, just like Jim said it would.

The next morning Jim and Cindy came over and we wanted them to see all the people and places in town that were important to me. Joey gave them the grand tour of our city. We drove by my mother's home where I had grown up as well as the schools I'd attended. We even surprised my parents' old friends, "Auntie June" and "Uncle Robert." Their daughters were visiting them that day and they were all excited to meet Jim and Cindy.

When we got back home, Dawn came over to visit, as did Joey's brother Tony and his wife Carol. I was very surprised that even my former mother-in-law, Mrs. Peters, came by to meet my father and Cindy. Mrs. Peters told them how happy she was that I had found them and how much she loved Joey and me. I was glad to hear her say that because sometimes I wasn't sure how she felt about us.

Mrs. Peters and I had a very tumultuous relationship. I can remember one time in particular that I stopped speaking to her for over a year after she hurt Brittany terribly with her cruel words. She called Brittany on her birthday and told her that since we changed her last name to Peters-Gowan (so that my daughters could share part of our last name), she no longer was her grandmother and would no longer celebrate birthdays or any holidays with gifts for her or India again. I even wondered why, after our estrangement, she decided to come over to meet my father. I didn't know if it was because she really cared or if she was just nosy. It didn't matter. I had forgiven her and was so happy that day that nothing could have ruined it. Mrs. Peters visited so long she almost missed her plane to South Carolina.

We all enjoyed a light lunch of jambalaya that I'd prepared and later had a big dinner at my favorite restaurant, The Olive Garden. By the end of our second night together, I was totally relaxed as Jim and I both had eased into our new relationship. I learned to like him while talking with him on the phone before we met, but now I knew I would grow to love the man I was talking with in person. I also grew closer and closer to Cindy with every moment we spent together. She was not related to me by blood and had her own children, yet she took the time to get to know me and treated me with the same love that Jim did. She is truly a very special woman. Our second night together was great, but I was really looking forward to spending the next day, Mother's Day, with all of my family. The next day would have been perfect if I still had my mother with me. I missed her desperately, but I knew that she was looking down at us from heaven and pleased with what she saw. She was with me in spirit.

Barb and Jim—first weekend meeting

Before visiting, Jim told me that even though he didn't go to church, he wanted to attend church with me on Mother's Day because he knew it would mean a lot to me. I was excited to be able to share my faith and my church family with him. He was pleasantly surprised with the outpouring of love and warmth. Everyone wanted to shake his hand and meet him. People commented that we look alike, even though I didn't see it. The sermon was wonderful as always and I was hoping that my pastor would have time to meet him.

At the close of service, much to my surprise, Pastor Wesley said, "Sister Barbara, please come and see me before you leave."

Jim said, "Is he talking about you?" He was amazed that in such a large congregation the pastor would take the time to meet him. Pastor Wesley told him how happy he was that we were being reunited and how special I was to the church. My father told him that he was proud to have me for a daughter. My father also met Dawn's dad, Mr. Marshall. Mr. Marshall told my dad that I was like a daughter to him and how much his family loved me.

My father was impressed with our pastor and the love in my church. He later told his sister Pat that if he lived nearby he might have jumped up and joined the church himself that day. He was never religious and held the opinion on church and religion that many scientists hold—that it's hard to believe something that can't be proved. One of his brothers was a minister, and Jim mentioned that he went to hear his first sermon to support him as well, but still didn't change his mind about organized religion. I knew I had to simply respect our differences.

After church, I realized that I no longer had to worry about having anxiety about my first reunion experience, as it had been a success. In fact, it was better than I ever imagined. I secretly wished my birth mother was as eager to meet me as my father was, but I knew I had to try to let that feeling go. I was having one of my best Mother's Days ever. Joey surprised me with a diamond ring and a beautiful amethyst ring since purple is my favorite color. I had my children, my husband, my birth father, my friends, and my church family to celebrate this extraordinary day with me. If my adoptive mother had been there she would have been so happy for me. She always wanted me to find my roots. My "Aunt June" said she thought my adoptive father would not have been so happy and would have had a hard time seeing me so excited to meet my birth father.

The one thing that was missing was being able to call Joanne to wish her a happy Mother's Day. Her husband was off on Sundays so I knew it wouldn't be a good idea to call. I sent her a card and a gift so she would know I was thinking about her. It was also her daughter Angie's first Mother's Day. I tried not to concentrate on that as I had other visits to look forward to.

Aunt Pat, Jim's older sister, and Aunt Loretta, his younger sister, told me that they wanted to visit me next. I was told repeatedly that Loretta was the one that I was most like. I wasn't nearly as nervous about their visit as I'd been about his, probably because they were women and we seemed very much alike. We bonded through our phone conversations and emails and I was eagerly anticipating their visit. Aunt Loretta lived in Maryland. She and her son, Steven, met my Aunt Pat in New York and they all came together by train.

When the train pulled into the station, I tried to picture the women that I was about to meet. A stunning woman who looked to be in her early 50s, but in reality was years older, got off the train with a younger woman and her son. I was amazed at their youthful appearance. Aunt Loretta looked like she was my age but in reality she was at least 10 years older. She was absolutely gorgeous. She is a fashion designer and was wearing one of her stunning, casual designs. I couldn't keep my eyes off Loretta. It was the first time I saw myself in another adult. We have the same facial expressions and noses. I was amazed at the resemblance. Aunt Pat was also very attractive and very classy. I hoped I would have their graceful-aging genes.

When we arrived home we were all pleasantly surprised that we had bought each other gifts. I received a beautiful nightgown, a crystal vase, and a plaque with a poem entitled "Niece." I had many created "Aunties" whom I loved dearly, but now I had some that shared my genes. This was a dream come true.

We immediately took to each other. Cindy told me on our first meeting that both Pat and Loretta loved to talk and when they were around there would be many different conversations going on at once. That is exactly what happened at my house. When Veronica, Dawn, and May, my mother-in-law, came over to meet them, there were so many conversations going on, it was hard to keep up with them all. It was an all girls day. We had a great time taking pictures and getting to know each other. I cooked a big soul-food dinner, which they said they thoroughly enjoyed. Loretta and Pat both shared my love of church and I looked forward to attending St. John's with them the next day.

Top—Veronica, May, Aunt Pat, Aunt Loretta, Brit, and Alena
Bottom—Barb and Dawn

Our church family welcomed them with open arms just as they had my father. Many people commented on the resemblance between Loretta and me. Pastor Wesley greeted them after church and they told him how much they'd enjoyed his sermon.

I learned to love them in the two short days of their visit. Loretta brought many family photos to show me. She said she saw a lot of her mother in me. That really meant a lot to me, especially since I would never be able to meet my grandmother, who'd died several years earlier. While going through the pictures, she pointed out that all of her brothers, except one, were in interracial marriages. She said, "We don't talk about race. It isn't an issue in our family." She added, "There are times in our family gatherings that I am the only black woman there." I thought it was odd that no one ever talked about race. It was great that everyone in the family was able to be colorblind, but I wondered if society treated them as if color weren't an issue. I also wondered if despite not talking about it, they thought about it. I knew it had always been an issue for me.

I once asked Jim how his family felt about his interracial relationships. His father grew up in the Deep South during a period when extreme racism was the law of the land. His father told him, "She will only hurt you," when he discovered that his son was involved with his first white girlfriend. Jim said he didn't understand what he'd meant because he was young and very naïve at the time. It seemed that his father was suspicious of white people for the same reasons my mother had been. He didn't want his son to get his feelings hurt or to be put in a situation where he may have to deal with racist comments. Confronting those issues in school and at work was hard enough, but putting yourself in a situation to have to deal with it in your personal life was just too much. His father eventually accepted Jim's and his brothers' interracial marriages.

Jim's father was of French Creole descent. Jim said that the French LeFlores were the slaveholders that gave them their name. Jim's dad was raised in Alabama and Jim lived there until he was about 10 years old. His father became a successful businessman, gaining postal contracts, and was able to move his family out of the South to upstate New York. He believed that education was the key to success, just as my mom had. Moving north would help them in gaining a great education.

Jim's dad told his children to emulate the white children in the area of education. Jim's white friends took Latin so he changed his classes to mirror theirs. Jim took pride in always being one of the top three students in his class. He explained to me how the students took a test every day and were then assigned seats based on their scores. He was always in one of the first three seats. That was a major accomplishment, especially since most of the other students' parents were professors or had a college education. Jim's parents did not, and he wasn't able to get as much help at home as the other kids did. He still excelled and made his parents proud. This was similar to my education. My mother told me I had to do better than the white kids in order to be "on an even playing field" with them. She was right; so was Jim's dad. It seemed that we both had a strong desire to make our parents proud of our academic achievements.

This was the case with all of the Leflore children. They all became successful despite the economic and educational obstacles they'd faced. Their family reminded me of the family described in the book *The Color of Water*, which I read at the recommendation of my therapist. It is the story of an interracial family in which all of the children overcame many obstacles to become educated and successful.

There was something else that I found noteworthy in my father's family. Every interracial family that I had known assimilated into the black community. It may have been because at one time, biracial children were considered simply black. Also, many white mothers were ostracized by their birth families while the black families welcomed them. The interracial LeFlore families, however, assimilated into the white community. This intrigued me. I wanted to know more about this but I didn't want to offend anyone by asking probing questions, especially since my aunt said no one in the family ever talked about race. I wasn't willing to open up that can of worms. I had more important things on my mind. I was thinking about the brother and sister that I had never met. That continued to be my greatest interest since finding my father.

I looked forward to meeting my half-siblings, but I got the sense that my sister Shelly was reluctant to meet me. This was very difficult for me since I had always dreamed of having a sister. I had to keep in mind that she was caught completely off guard by the revelation of a sister at this point in her life, and may not feel the same way I did. She grew up with a biological family and I realized she couldn't possibly understand how much our potential relationship would mean to me. I hoped she would eventually want to get to know me. I decided to be patient and not call her. I thought she needed to be ready to talk to me and would call when the time was right for her. I was so excited when she called me on May 16, 2004.

We had a wonderful conversation that showed me that my fears were all unfounded. Her voice sounded eerily similar to our father's voice. We talked about our children and husbands as well as our jobs and interests. I told her about my adoptive family and she talked to me about her life after her parents' divorce when she lived with her mom and brother. I found out that after her parents divorced, her mother left New York and got a job working in Westfield, Massachusetts. That was strange enough, but what was stranger still was that she ended up living in my hometown of Springfield because her mom wanted them to live in an environment near other black kids. I was told that their mom always put her children's needs before her own. Springfield is a large city, and what was so amazing to me was not only that they lived in the same city as me, but also that their home was only about two miles from my childhood home, in a neighbor-hood I knew well and rode past every day.

The most astonishing piece of information came next. She told me that her brother Randy attended Kiley Jr. High School, my school, at the same time that I was there. I was shocked! I thought, "What a small world." It seemed unbeliev-able to me that my biological parents were both from New York and that my bio-logical siblings not only lived within two miles of my home but my brother walked the same hallways at the same time in the same school as I did. Then I thought about the fact that I had always been attracted to tall, light-skinned guys. I thought to myself, "It's a good thing I never met or dated him." This alone sounded like a good argument for open adoption records. Surprisingly, Shelly also told me that her mother worked at the same place where Joey's mother worked during the time they lived in Massachusetts. Everyone I spoke with always had such wonderful things to say about their mom. She was always described as a loving, caring person. Even after their divorce, she and Jim remained good friends until she died of cancer.

Shelly and I talked about many things that first night on the phone; we not only discussed family and careers but also our friends and the topic of adoption. She told me a story about one of her uncles. He was adopted and had found his birth mother. When he contacted her, she answered his questions then asked him not to call her again. Shelly said that she felt really bad for him. Because of this, I assumed that she would be sensitive to my feelings, knowing that rejection from birth families can be very painful.

We exchanged contact information so that we could continue to get acquainted by email and photos until we could meet. I was so excited that she had called. My father was also elated that she called me. I immediately looked for Randy's picture in my junior high school yearbook after we'd got off the phone. But the old photo was very blurry. I would have to wait to see him in person.

Jim said that Randy was a lot like me. He also told me that Randy hadn't called me yet because he wanted to let me meet my father first. My father said that Randy was so impulsive that he knew once he talked to me he would probably say, "How about I just drive out to meet you?" I thought it was very considerate that he waited until I'd met Jim before he called me. Randy called me on May 22, 2004, and we talked for an hour and a half. He said, "How about I ride down next weekend?" Before even meeting me he said that he considered me his sister and if I ever needed anything he would be there for me. I appreciated his caring spirit.

The next weekend Randy arrived on his new motorcycle with his girlfriend. He talked about the family's history and his life and relationships with the

LeFlore family. I enjoyed hearing about the family interactions and different personalities. I began to see that we were, indeed, very much alike. We are both very open, honest, outgoing, and talkative. We also place a lot of value on family. I was touched by the fact that after he was divorced, he moved to where his ex-wife lived to be close to his sons. He lives right next to their school and is involved in every aspect of their lives. He expressed his desire to move back to New York when his children graduate, to be closer to his father. He explained to me that Jim took care of his mother for years before she died. Jim didn't want to put her in a nursing home because he didn't trust that she would be well cared for because of her race. Randy told me that he wants to be close enough to his dad so that he can do as his father did and care for him in his later years if he isn't able to care for himself. I learned a lot about my brother's character in those few hours that we visited. I was also happy to hear my children say that they thought we looked alike.

Next I had a visit with my sister. Shelly suggested that we meet at a restaurant that was halfway between our homes, right off the highway. During this 45-minute ride, I became more and more nervous. I couldn't believe that I was going to finally meet my sister. Our personalities were very different and I hoped we would like each other. My good friend Veronica and I are very different yet our differences compliment each other. I hoped the same would be true for Shelly and me. We got acquainted over a very long lunch. She proved to be a very nice person, just more reserved than Randy. We agreed to keep in touch and took pictures together. She and Randy are much taller than I am, but I could see similarities between Shelly and me just as I had with Randy and me. We all seemed to have the pointy Leflore nose. She also had long, curly hair like mine. I'd always wished I had a sister, and now I did. I couldn't wait to share my visit and my first photographs of my siblings with everyone.

Joey suggested that we visit my father in New York for Father's Day. Jim thought it was a great idea. It started out as a small event and grew into a big family reunion. My Aunt Loretta, her boyfriend Bill, and her son drove up from Silver Springs, Maryland. Randy drove up with his two sons and his girlfriend. My Uncle Ray and his girlfriend also came up and I met him for the first time. I was disappointed that Shelly couldn't come, but at least we got to know each other during our first visit together. My dad put us up in a nice hotel overlooking Lake Ontario. The children had a wonderful time in the pool and the Jacuzzi and loved meeting their cousins and uncle for the first time. Randy's boys were about the same age as India and Brittany and they got along great together.

I learned more about my family's history as we looked at old photo albums. There were photos of my siblings as they were growing up and younger pictures of my dad and my aunts and uncles. I also learned about their mother's brother, Preston Goode, who was over one hundred years old. I continued to be amazed at the accomplishments of the LeFlore family. There was a judge, a mayor, and even a family member with a street named after him. I was fascinated to read an old pamphlet from 1972 about John L. LeFlore, who was Alabama's first black candidate for the U.S. Senate. He had many accomplishments in the areas of civil rights and public service. While working with the NAACP from 1935-1956, he worked on initiatives that investigated many lynchings, repealed Jim Crow laws that previously denied Pullman and dining-car services to blacks on eight major railroads, and worked to stop discrimination that denied blacks employment as clerks and carriers in the Mobile post offices. He helped to start the War Manpower Training Program to get blacks employed in skilled capacities at shipyards during World War II. He also fought job discrimination in public schools, and for desegregation of buses and parks. My birth father's dad was also remarkable. He was able to gain contracts within the post office that helped him to move his family from Alabama to upstate New York in his quest for a better education and quality housing for his family.

That was a very special Father's Day weekend. I learned a lot about that part of my family tree. We had a big barbeque one day and on another day all went out to a nice restaurant. We began to feel like a real family after that weekend.

A few weeks later, on July third, Randy invited us to a cookout at his home. This time Shelly and her family were there. This was another first—the first time I was with both of my siblings. We took a photo that was later used in a story written for our local newspaper. Our children enjoyed playing together and swimming in the pool. We listened to all kinds of music and had a great time. Once again, I felt like I really belonged there.

My boys then posed an interesting question. They wanted to know how Randy's sons and Shelly's sons could be related to us as they all looked white. I explained to them that Shelly and Randy both married people who were white, and that is why the children looked white. Only a child would ask a question like that without blinking an eye. Not only were they meeting relatives we never knew before, but also they were seeing many skin colors in one family. It was all very interesting to them. I explained to them that God loves people for what is inside, not for the outside color of their skin. Once their questions were answered, they went on as children do, just happy to be playing with their new cousins. The day ended with us driving home that evening to attend a gospel concert at Six Flags New England featuring Fred Hammond. I couldn't imagine a better way to celebrate my wedding anniversary.

Although I had a great few months meeting many relatives, I was looking forward to some quiet time with my husband and children as we took off for a two-week Florida vacation. I felt I hadn't spent much quality time with them with all of the emailing and telephone conversations with my "birth people," as I often called them. While in Florida, I had time for reflection and prayer as well as fun and relaxation with the kids at the pool and by the ocean. We played games, rode bikes, watched movies, and went sightseeing. It was the first time the boys went on the rides Splash Mountain and Space Mountain at Disney World. They were too small to ride them on our previous visits. The girls hung out with their friends at the clubhouse. Brittany discovered a teenage dance club at Universal's City Walk. While I was away, both Joanne and Jim had birthdays. I made sure to remember their birthdays to let them know how much I appreciated them.

When I returned from Florida, Joanne shared with me what a good time she had visiting her son, his new baby, and all of their family in New York. There was a part of me that was hurt because I felt like I was still a deep, dark secret where her family was concerned. I thought that this must be how a mistress feels. I had to sneak around to communicate with someone I cared about. I thought she was ashamed of our relationship.

I decided to focus more on my blessings than on what I was missing. I was realizing that it is our thoughts that control our actions and moods. Experiencing joy comes from focusing on joyful things. Every cup can be perceived as half-full or half-empty. I chose to see the cups in my life as half-full, and looked forward to my birth father's next visit.

On Jim's next visit, he stayed with us for one night, and then the next day we all went to Randy's house for a lobster feast. I was excited about spending time with Jim, my siblings, and all of our children. During our visit to Randy's, we were playing cards in the yard when a man came down the stairs from the deck. I didn't recognize him, but I knew he was probably a relative. This man turned out to be my Uncle Walter, Jim's youngest brother. Jim said he didn't have as much contact with Walter because there was a large age difference between them. He explained that in some large families, some siblings are closer than others. Since I was an only child, this was a strange concept to me. I wanted siblings so badly that I couldn't understand having them and not being close to all of them.

Uncle Walter heard that I was at Randy's and came to his house so that he could meet me. I felt honored that he went out of his way to meet me. We got along very well. His personality was more like Randy's and mine than some of the other members of the family. I was happy to be surrounded by my new family, who made me feel so comfortable and welcome. This was also the first time both of my siblings, my dad, and I were all together. We were able to snap our first photo together. I now had met almost all of the family members, except for my two uncles who lived in Maryland. They would be next on my reunion list.

My Aunt Loretta invited us to visit her in Maryland. She wanted me to experience life in her world. Her brother Ivens had just bought a new home and was going to have a family barbeque for us. I was excited to meet him but was even more excited to meet his son, Michael, whom everyone said was one of the nicest people I would ever meet. They were right. He was warm, friendly, kind, and a joy to talk to. He was part Asian and the combination of his African-American and Asian features also made him strikingly handsome. He came with his girlfriend, who was equally nice. Ivens was a plastic surgeon and I didn't expect that he would be as down to earth as he was. He also had the most charming wife with the cutest British accent.

On our first night, Aunt Loretta and I stayed up into the wee hours of the morning sharing all of our most important life experiences. I felt a closeness to her that surpassed all of my wildest dreams. I treasured my relationship with her. Her son Steven and my daughter Brittany were close in age, with similar interests, and they clicked, too.

The next day, more visitors arrived. First, a few of Aunt Loretta's friends came by to meet me. After just a short period, it seemed like we were all old friends. Uncle Lou also came by with his wife. He was unlike the rest of the brothers. He was a minister and shared my love for the Lord. It was nice to be able to talk about church and my faith with him since I often felt like I made some people uncomfortable when talking about my religion. Uncle Lou was also the only one of the brothers who was married to a black woman. He seemed to be cut from a different mold. He encouraged me to continue to be proud of my faith, my race, and my culture, no matter how it made others feel. He encouraged me to be true to myself. I appreciated that.

Later that evening, Steven and Brittany rented movies and offered to watch the boys so that we adults could enjoy some of the DC area nightlife. Loretta and her boyfriend Bill took Joey and I to a great house party in an upscale neighborhood. There were so many people there, laughing and dancing and having a great time. By the time the weekend was over, we were all exhausted. I hated to leave but we had to go.

Barb and Auntie Loretta

As we drove home, I realized that all along I had had the blood ties with the LeFlore family that made us relatives, but now we were beginning to share the life experiences that really make us a family. I began thinking about the upcoming annual family picnic with my adoptive dad's family.

The Miller picnic was held every August at a local park. Our family had grown so much that I didn't know most of the younger members of the family. I was much closer with all of them when I was a younger child. Nevertheless, we looked forward to going every year. I was also looking forward to sharing the news that I located my biological parents. Some of my relatives were excited for me; others were not. I kept hearing the same comments from relative after relative. They all mirrored what my cousin Steven told me, "Barbie, we never saw you as adopted—just a Miller, like the rest of us!" Despite my own feelings of never really belonging anywhere, I came to realize that they had accepted me as one of their own all along. We may not have had the blood ties, but we had many shared experiences and love that made us family.

As the summer came to an end, I looked forward to the two other special events I had planned before having to return to work. Two of my favorite singers were touring in my area. Prince was on his Musicology tour, and I had front row tickets. Veronica, Mike, Joey, and I drove to Boston for the concert. It was absolutely amazing. The energy in that building was indescribable as he sang new and old songs alike. As my walk with the Lord developed, I had a hard time listening to some of the more explicit lyrics from his earlier recordings. Prince, as he developed his own walk with God, stopped swearing and stopped singing his more sexually explicit songs. The best part about the concert was that Prince bent down and shook my hand! That reminded me of when I saw the group The Time in concert and Jerome bent down and lifted me up on the stage to dance "The Bird" with him. I didn't think anything could top that—but shaking Prince's hand definitely did. Within a few weeks, we also were able to attend another Peabo Bryson concert. Meeting all of my new relatives, hanging out with my old relatives, and then attending those two concerts all in one summer left me on an emotional high. But, as they say, "What goes up, must come down." My emotional high wouldn't last for long.

11

Learning and Growing

As fall approached, I began to feel a little sad. I missed all of the contact with my father's family and it made me realize how much I missed not meeting my birth mother or her daughter. I was feeling more and more like her dark, little secret. It just didn't seem fair. I was grateful for the kindness she had shown me, and the nice things she said to me, but I just couldn't understand why she wasn't ready to see me. Once again I felt like I had to think about what was best for her and her family. I wanted to scream, "Why won't she think about what I need?" I talked to my therapist about it and she thought that the secrecy and inability of my birth mother to talk about me to family members was probably largely due to the problems that many birth mothers deal with when giving up a child for adoption. She stressed the need for me to be patient and understanding.

Another thing I didn't understand was why she didn't want to tell her son. After all, he had dated a black girl. Angie also said that she accidentally slipped and told him that their mom had given up a child for adoption around the time he was having his first child. Joanne said that he never mentioned that to her and he probably didn't remember that part of their conversation.

It was easier to share my feelings with Angie because we mostly communicated by email. She said that she wasn't a "phone person" so we spoke infrequently on the phone. She was always genuinely nice, but I wished Joanne and Angie wanted to meet me as badly as I wanted to meet them. I had to realize that they never missed the same kind of family connections that I had missed. In fact, Joanne and her husband seemed to have the perfect nuclear family with the biological connections that I always wanted. Angie said that she was curious about me, but I don't think she felt she was missing anything by not knowing me.

Whenever I hung up the phone after talking to her, I would think, "I hope she was happy to talk to me," or "I should have asked her this or that," or "I wonder if she is just being nice." I was often careful about what I chose to talk about with her for fear of making her feel uncomfortable. It was hard for me to just relax and enjoy our conversations or to just enjoy the process of getting to know each other.

I received the comfort I needed by talking things over with my close friends, and in prayer. Once again, I kept reminding myself that I needed to appreciate my glass being half-full rather than half-empty. I dreamed about finding my birth family for most of my life; at least I was able to communicate with my biological family members. I never wanted to push myself on anyone or put myself in a position where I would have to deal with feeling unwanted again.

In my attempt to navigate through this unfamiliar territory, I sought support and guidance through various adoption web sites and books. I began to read stories about adoption reunions in order to learn through the experiences of others. It was helpful to know that others adoptees shared many of same feelings I had.

A particularly helpful article that I found on adoption.com forums entitled "Relationship Stages After Reunion" by Carol P. Turesk, explained some of the changing emotions experienced by members of the adoption triad—that is, adoptees, biological parents, and adoptive parents—during the reunion process. It discussed five distinct stages:

- The first stage is the Honeymoon. The parties feel they are on top of the world, finding similarities and common interests, catching up on each other's lives, exchanging photos, gifts, and letters. There may be a little uncertainty about how they will relate to each other and their respective families.

- The second stage is the Time Out. This is a time of evaluation often accompanied by confusion and frustration. Feelings may be hurt during this stage. Problems can arise in relationships during this time.

- The third stage is the Showdown. Fear of rejection may be a concern and confrontations can develop to address the status of the relationships.

- The fourth stage is Disengagement. Parties may become distant because of rigid expectations or vast differences in life stages and interests.

- The final stage is Solidifying. Negotiations between the parties are made and there is growth in the relationships. This stage may continue throughout the relationship.

Not everyone experiences all of the stages and they may not necessarily happen in that exact sequence. I was happy to learn that it was normal for things to change in that way. My therapist also gave me reality checks as needed. She helped me consider the needs of my birth families as well as my own. Sometimes I thought it wasn't fair that I had to work so hard to respect everyone else's feelings, especially Joanne's. At first, Joanne and I talked daily, and then as time went on the talks went to weekly, then monthly, then just on special occasions. I tried to give her space when I thought she needed it and tried not to say anything that would hurt her feelings. There were times when I wanted to say, "What about me? I didn't have a choice." I wondered why she wasn't thinking of my needs.

That reminded me of the quote by The Reverend Keith C. Griffin that I found on an adoption web site: "Adoption is the only trauma in the world where the victims are expected by the whole of society to be grateful." I have heard many times since finding my birth mother that I need to respect her need for privacy, give her time, give her space, understand her feelings, and let her be in the driver's seat. I should just be grateful that I was adopted or simply grateful to be alive.

We are expected to be so grateful to our adoptive parents for rescuing us that we are often made to feel uncaring or selfish if we choose to search for our biological parents. I am grateful that my adoptive mother never made me feel that way. In fact, she told me that when I married Pete, she tried to find my birth mother so that she could see me get married; but she was unsuccessful.

I am grateful for my life, my family, and my friends, but that doesn't negate the feelings of loss I have felt for most of my life. The sense of loss that many adoptees experience is generally not understood by society. We aren't given the opportunity to mourn our loss because it is a more ambiguous loss than that felt at the death of a loved one. There have been many studies done and literature written about loss through death and dying. Society is compassionate and understanding about the need for comfort and the support required to work through the grief process until a stage of healing and acceptance is reached after a loved one dies. But there does not seem to be the same attention paid to the sense of loss that adoptees experience.

One adoptee I spoke with was able to put my feelings into words. She said, "In expecting us to feel grateful and specially chosen, it prevents us from having the full range of healthy feelings that are attached to adoption—feeling grateful might be part of that, but feeling alone and that no one truly understands your needs or experience might also be part of it for some adoptees. Sometimes, adoptees can feel we must be ultra-sensitive to the needs of others to ensure that our connections and relationships with them survive." She went on to say that, "Perhaps some adoptees feel that they don't fully or legitimately belong to any family system—that we are, to differing degrees, either invited, claimed (as in a search process), or chosen (as in an adopted family). Further, for some adoptees, there is no family system to which they feel connected (except the ones we create) where we just exist and no one questions it as 'real' (including ourselves) and where we trust our membership is permanent and can't be undone."

I agreed with her words and have always felt like I didn't belong and that I was just blending into other people's families. Maybe that is the reason I chose to have so many children of my own, to create a family I felt was really mine.

Despite having comfort in knowing that my feelings of loss and isolation were validated by other adoptees, I didn't feel that anyone in my birth family could really understand what I was going through. I couldn't make them understand nor did I try to; however, I did try to understand the wide range of emotions they were experiencing.

I continued to search adoption web sites for books and blogs to learn more from other members of the adoption triad. One community member mentioned a book called *Birthmothers* that helped her see things from a different point of view. It related stories of different birth mothers and how their lives were forever changed after giving up a child for adoption. Some women had many children, subconsciously trying to replace the child they gave up. They found, however, that one child could never replace another. The pain of that loss remains. Others never wanted to have more children. Some had difficult relationships in general and some were able to move on without much difficulty.

They shared similar issues but handled them differently depending on their support systems and their own personality types. Many feared that they would lose the families that they acquired after the adoption if their secret got out. Having lost one child, many birth mothers feared suffering yet another loss. Some even feared losing the adopted child again if they reconnected. Many birth mothers suffered from low self-esteem, guilt, shame, and anxiety. Some of the women were told to just get on with their lives and forget about the child. Decisions were made for them and they were convinced they were doing what was in the best interest of the child. Most didn't receive counseling or support to deal with all of the complicated issues related to adoption. Still, most of the birth mothers said they would be willing to experience fear and emotional turmoil for a chance to know the child they gave up for adoption.

I also read an article called "Practical Advice for Reuniting Families" by Linda Back McKay, which offered important tips for reunions. She gave a list that included:

Be yourself

Be resourceful (finding out how other families handled reunions)

Be sensitive to the needs and feelings of others

Be a good listener

Be patient

Be honest (communicate openly. If you want to know something then ask and be understanding)

The one that was most difficult for me was being patient. I had waited 40 years for this. The author said she had been reunited with her son for almost twelve years and they were still getting to know each other.

McKay also said that it was important to remember that many people—not just the child and the parent—are affected by adoption reunions. I tried to keep that in mind, especially when thinking of Joanne. She had children, grandchildren, and extended family members who could all be affected by my re-entry into her life. According to McKay, it is easy to make the reunion the central focus of life but it is important to remember the significance of the other people in your life. You must also remember that no matter how the reunion and relationships turn out, everyone is in charge of his or her own happiness.

Another writer said that reunion is like a journey to a foreign country where one doesn't know the customs or speak the language. This author compared the searcher to a truck traveling 90 miles per hour and the person who is found is taken by surprise and without the same kind of momentum. When the two energies meet, an emotional collision occurs. The searcher can't slow down, while the person found has the wind knocked out of him and is gasping for air. Both parties will never be the same. This writer stressed that all relationships evolve over time and that the reunion mantra should be "We have the rest of our lives to resolve this."

I have this statement posted in my office at work, along with "Let Go and Let God," to help me focus on being patient. I became aware that I needed to focus less of my attention on my "birthpeople" and more on my nuclear family. It was a new season with new struggles.

We were all excited for the new school year. Brittany was chosen to attend a new school through a school choice program. The school system was known to be one of the best in Western Massachusetts, so we decided to give it a try. She was sent to a high school in a predominantly white, upper-class suburb where there were very few children of color. She didn't want to go, but I thought it would be best for her academically. We thought she would also learn to adapt to a different environment. This wasn't the case. It was difficult for her to focus on her schoolwork because of what she felt was a hostile environment. She was called "nigger" repeatedly and harassed by the other students. I filed a complaint with the dean of students. The harassment continued, so I told her that she would finish the school year then return to one of our local high schools. It was hard for me to see her go to school depressed, with her self-esteem shattered. She was unable to maintain her usual honor-roll grades. The dean of students, who I'd thought would try to help Brittany, said to me, "Maybe this just isn't the place for your daughter." Brittany didn't feel welcome there and neither did I. If it weren't for a counselor named Bob and her boyfriend, Vianchi, I don't think she would have been able to keep her sanity while in that school. I realized the decision to send her to that school was a bad one. Unfortunately, parenting isn't an exact science and we make mistakes and have to learn along the way. I've often wished life could be picture-perfect with no racism, sexism, or "religionisms."

There were very few times I felt we could have a world like that. However, one day at Dawn's house made me see it as possible. She and her husband Gerald had just bought a beautiful home overlooking a plush, green lawn on the top of a hill. The group of people who attended her housewarming party was an eclectic mix of all races and religions. After enjoying an afternoon of good food and fellowship, we all began to have an intellectual conversation about various religions. Dawn's mother's friends and family were Jewish; Dawn's father's extended family was Muslim. My family and some of her other friends and family members were Christian. We all shared a great conversation filled with the loving attitude of accepting each other's views. We made the observation that if more people of differing races and religions could have intelligent conversation without hate and anger, we could all finally live in peace. We are born free of hate and prejudice. Those are things we are taught. I believe that we should spend more time teaching love. Unfortunately, our little gathering of friends doesn't reflect global society.

In October 2004, I joked with my therapist that I would need an appointment after my approaching birthday because I would feel like dying if my birth mother didn't remember it. She told me that my birthday might be very difficult for her, as it is for many birth mothers, and she may not call if she can't handle it. The anticipation of the day became very stressful. I would often cause myself undue stress with holidays in general. I'd put a lot of emphasis on the particular day and then feel let down if it didn't go just right. I have heard that this is one of the causes of the increased incidence of depression, illness, and suicide around the holidays.

I thought about my fortieth birthday the year before. It was memorable. Porsche and my boys made my day special with songs and cards. Joey surprised me with a digital camcorder, which we took to New York City, where we went to celebrate. We rode our bicycle-built-for-two from Harlem on the north end of Manhattan island to Ground Zero at the southern end, and back through Central Park. The day was a slice of heaven for us. When I returned, I enjoyed my traditional girlfriend lunches with my closest friends.

The night before this birthday, Joey gave me an iPod. I didn't even know what it was, but he told me it was the hottest, new technology and I would love it. I could program all of my favorite songs into it and take it to the gym or for walks without carrying a big CD case. I was excited to get started programming my music. I think he gave it to me the night before so I would have something to occupy my mind in case my birth mother forgot my birthday.

My birth father told me to keep an eye on the mail for my gift. I knew he would have a nice surprise for me as he shared my sentimental nature. It isn't the size or the value of the gift that is important, but rather the time and the thought behind it that makes it so special. I was pleasantly surprised when I got to work and found the email that Angie had sent. It included an e-card with recent family photos attached. That put a smile on my face first thing in the morning.

During lunch, Joey called and told me he was on his way to my job. I felt the same anticipation I'd felt when we were waiting for the paternity test results from Jim. He came to the door bubbling with excitement. He had flowers that were delivered to my house from my father and Cindy. He also had a long thin box that was about three-feet long, and another large, square box. I was so filled with joy I thought I would explode. Jim told me that I should never lose my refreshing, kid-like excitement at receiving gifts. I told him I wouldn't.

I opened up the long box first. It held long-stemmed lilies in a fancy vase from my Aunt Pat. She did everything with such class. Next I opened the square box. It was from my Aunt Loretta. She'd made me a shawl, which was just perfect for me. The label said *Leflore by Design*. It was one of her special designs. I didn't think the day could get much better after all of that. But it did.

Barb wearing shawl with birthday flowers

My sister Shelly sent me a card and my brother Randy called me before I even had a chance to get home. When I finally made it home, I found a big, brown box on my dining room table. JJ, John, and Porsche were watching TV in the living room and I asked them where the box came from. They didn't know. How silly of me, they were little kids. I looked at the return label expecting it to be from my father. It was from Las Vegas. My birth mother remembered.

I opened the box like it was my only gift under the tree on Christmas. I was tearing paper and spilling the packing on the floor. Inside was a boxful of hand-crocheted items she'd made for me. She made an angel, a doily, sun catchers, purple candleholders, and purple potholders. Not only did she remember my birthday but also she remembered some of my favorite things and my favorite color. She included a recent photo of herself and a beautiful card with a nice message. This was the first thing I had in her handwriting. These gifts meant so much to me because I knew she'd spent a lot of time making them just for me.

Before the thrill subsided, the phone rang.

"Hello," I answered.

"Hi, Barb," said the very familiar voice on the other end.

"Hi, Joanne. I am so happy to hear from you," I said.

"I was calling to wish you a happy birthday. How was your day today?" she asked.

"I had a great day and it's even better now that I am talking to you."

"Did you receive my package today?"

"Yes. I just made a big mess in the living room tearing open the box to get to the gifts inside."

"I hope you liked the things I made for you. You said that you liked candles. That's why I made the candleholders. I also thought you would like the angel. I like sun catchers and potholders and that is why I made them. I made the potholders purple since it is your favorite color. The doily took the longest to make."

"They were all beautiful and they meant so much to me because I know you made them with your own hands." I then paused and continued with, "I was afraid you would forget my birthday."

"Oh, Barb, I remember your birthday every year," she said.

That was music to my ears and what I'd always longed to hear. As we continued catching up on the recent events of our lives, I thought to myself, "This is the best birthday I have ever had!"

The next day I received a package from my birth father with a pair of beautiful earrings inside. From our first meeting, he could tell that I loved jewelry. I shared my great news with my closest friends. I was able to reflect upon all of the special blessings I had received during the last seven months of my life.

I felt like Dorothy in the Wizard of Oz. I had been searching for something to make me feel complete. After finding my birth family, I took a long, hard look at my life and realized that I had always been blessed. For the majority of my life, I longed to find my "real" family. I found them, and yes I felt, and continue to feel, loved. Yet through it all, I came to realize that the people I had in my life all along had always loved me and considered me part of their family, despite not being related by blood. I was the only one who seemed to be focused on that issue. For everyone else, it was a non-issue. I'd been so busy looking for what I felt was missing, that I didn't take the time to count the blessings I already had.

My blessings include four beautiful, bright children of my own, a loving husband and stepdaughter, as well as caring and devoted friends. I had adoptive parents who loved me and gave me all they had to give. They raised me to become a strong, independent person. Despite losing them, I am grateful for the time we had together. Instead of focusing on how sad I am about losing Michelle, I try to remember what a joy it was to have her in my life. I probably would've never been able to have the close friendships that I have with Veronica, Dawn, Dana, or Alicia, if not for learning what true, unconditional friendship was from Michelle.

Instead of dwelling on the hurtful and difficult times in my life, I now try to focus on what I learned from them. I would never have developed courage and strength if not for the trials I was able to endure. Being able to see the goodness in all shades of people may not have been possible for me if not for the rainbow of loving people I was blessed to have in my life. Finally, I would never have known the peace that comes from my faith in God if not for Pastor Wesley, St. John's Congregational Church, and my church family.

PART V
Fulfilling My Purpose

12

Enlarging My Territory

o o o o o o o o o o o o o o o o o o o o o o o o o o o o o o o o

Oh, that You would bless me indeed, and enlarge my territory, that Your hand would be with me, and that You would keep me from evil that I may not cause pain.

—The Prayer of Jabez

At St. John's we were taught the Prayer of Jabez and its lessons related to blessings and enlarging territory. I have been blessed with finding my birth family and with finding peace on my spiritual journey. I looked forward with anticipation to enlarging my territory with the awareness that I had to be still in prayer. I also had to be willing to go into unfamiliar territory if that was where God led me. Lessons from the Prayer of Jabez include:

- We are blessed so that we can bless others.

- We ask God to bless us "indeed" to ask for the largest blessing that God can give; leaving it entirely up to God when, where, and how to bless us.

- "Enlarging territory" is about expanding our opportunities and our effect on others in such a way that we touch more lives for God's glory.

- God's hand on us does not make us great but shows God's greatness through us.

- The request to be kept from evil is so that we will not have to fight against it. It is a brilliant strategy for sustaining a blessed life.

After living through the pain and emptiness of not knowing and not fitting in, my journey toward self-actualization, and my search for my biological family, my territory became enlarged by contact with other adoptees who had lived through the same feeling of isolation that I'd experienced. We have touched each other's lives in ways that are difficult to explain. I have been truly blessed to be a part of so many people's lives, and I wanted to continue by being a blessing to others. To quote Reverend Dr. Howard John Wesley, "Do you know what you call it when your pain blesses someone else? We call that a ministry." I had previously been ashamed of many of my childhood problems regarding race and my adoption. I didn't want to expose my weaknesses and vulnerabilities. As time went on, I realized that our wounds could become a witness to others. It was OK to show others what the Lord has delivered me from. In one of Pastor Wesley's sermons he said, "It's one thing to be delivered from something but its another to be so delivered that you can testify without being worried about what folks will think or say about you." He helped me to realize that I could finally stop being ashamed of my scars.

As I began to share my story with coworkers and share my testimony with church members, I was overwhelmed with the number of adoptees who approached me, wanting to find their own birth families. My territory was enlarged and my blessing did become a blessing to others. I was able to share information with them and help them to find their birth families.

Carol, a coworker, came to visit me and to ask questions about how to search for her birth family. I referred her to Kinsolving Investigations and she found her biological family within a couple of weeks. Her birth mother was elderly and grateful to have been found, since she had also been searching for Carol, with no luck. Carol has developed very close relationships with her seven siblings and other family members who have welcomed their new "Aunt Carol." She shares many family celebrations with them, but she has yet to inquire about the identity of her birth father. She is satisfied with her current relationships for now.

Equally important is the bond that Carol and I have developed. We were able to share feelings about being adopted without the fear of being judged for being ungrateful for our adoptive families. Her husband is also of mixed race and we were able to discuss how biracial people feel in this predominantly white country. Carol and I were able to share each phase of our reunions and how they were affecting our lives. We began scrapbooking to chronicle our lives and our newly found family members.

When I gave my testimony in church, it seemed like those in search of biological family members came out of the woodwork. One woman, Kim, was part of a prayer group I attended. Her children also attended the school where I work as a nurse. When I first told her my story, she said, "I guess I just never had that burning desire like you did." She had never searched, even though she was curious about the origins of her birth and also wondered if her brother, who was also adopted, was her biological brother.

She never discussed her feelings with any of her adoptive-family members because she didn't want to hurt their feelings. Although she had suppressed these feelings, she had the same questions that most adoptees have such as "Who do I look like?" and "I wonder why I was given up" and "I wonder what my medical history is" and "I wonder if I have any siblings."

As time went on and we discussed her feelings, she decided to send for her non-identifying information. She was amazed at all of the information she received. There were letters that her mother had written from jail where she was sent prior to Kim's birth. Kim learned she had four siblings, two were placed with their biological father and two were placed elsewhere. She discovered that her birth mother was murdered when she was only thirty years old. In her information file, she read a heart-wrenching story of how two of her siblings, an unnamed boy and a girl named Elaine, were found abandoned in a cellar with only a curdled bottle of milk between the two of them. She realized then that she needed to find her siblings. Both of us were very concerned about those two children who'd been left in that cellar.

With help from a person that Kim calls her angel, she finally received information about a brother named Marvin, the unnamed boy in the cellar. When she received her brother's phone number, she came into my office to make the call. With the same feelings of anxiety and excitement I had during my first call to my birth mother, Kim dialed the number. No answer. She decided to leave him a message.

Because I usually have a camera with me and I like to capture everything on film, I suggested we take photos of those precious moments of discovery. Within ten minutes, he'd returned her call. She was grinning from ear to ear. They got to know each other right before my eyes. The best part was that he was just as excited to meet her, as she was to meet him. We were able to capture it all on film.

A few days after locating Marvin, she located the two siblings who'd been sent to live with their father in Florida. They all now lived in New York. By the end of the week, her sister Elaine, the other child in the cellar, had also been found, in Las Vegas. Some of the siblings didn't know about each other. None of them knew about Kim. They were amazed and grateful that the one sibling none of them knew anything about had reunited them all.

When the two siblings came from New York, they brought along their father, who was able to shed light on their birth mother's life. He explained that she was emotionally abandoned by her family and became a drifter. She had a very difficult life. Kim said that it was refreshing to hear about her mother's struggles in life from someone who truly loved her. I was excited to meet all of them as well. Kim and I took many photos to use in a scrapbook she would later make of her new family members.

Another woman, who wanted to help her fiancé find his birth mother, also approached me in church. I gave her information about how to conduct a search. Within a couple of weeks, his birth mother was also found. He also learned that he has many siblings. They are all just beginning to define their relationships. We are now in the process of helping yet another biracial adopted woman who shares some of the same problems and conflicts that I wrestled with growing up.

As my territory became more and more enlarged, I realized I needed more information on how to effectively help others. I called Sherrie Eldridge who was one of my favorite adoption authors. She suggested I start a support group, since there were none in my area. As God would have it, we have developed an informal support group. If it is God's will, we will establish a more formal group and seek outside members.

It was at this time that I decided to share my story on a larger scale. I wrote an article for the Adoption Week e-magazine that I frequently read. It was titled "Lessons From My Journey." I also began contemplating writing this book. Sherrie gave me information on the writing process, information about publishing, and the encouragement to share my story as a ministry to others. She then led me to Michelle Hughes, an adoption attorney who works closely with not only adoptive families but also those in the multicultural community. This definitely was taking me out of my comfort zone. This is when I remembered what Minister Angela Lewis once told me. She said, "You never know where God will lead you."

Another opportunity for increasing my territory came during the first week of November 2004. I was reading the Adoption Week e-magazine on-line and noticed they were asking for members of the adoption triad to assist in portraying more positive views of adoption to society. I wanted to do my part.

One of the negative depictions of adopted children is that we are seen as "those poor, unwanted children" rescued by our adoptive parents. In reality there are many reasons children are placed with adoptive families. It is not always because we were unwanted. There are many jokes made about how adopted children don't seem to fit into their adoptive families. The jokes even include biological children. Whenever a member of the family doesn't look or act like the rest, they are told jokingly, "Maybe you were adopted." Even worse, if a biological child is seen as the black sheep of the family or the child that doesn't seem to get the love and attention that the other children get, they get the "you must have been adopted" comment. I remember watching the movie *Dodgeball* in which a similar joke was made toward a character. Everyone in the room laughed. Most adoptees, however, don't think that kind of joke is funny. Before the wave of celebrity adoptions, another common assumption about adoption was that only people who couldn't have "children of their own" chose adoption—it was the last resort. I wanted to share my points of view in regard to adoption.

Within a week of reading the Adoption Week e-magazine, a childhood friend wrote an article about my journey for our local newspaper. It was in recognition of November being National Adoption Awareness Month. The reporter was a member of my church family, and a special childhood friend, so I trusted her with my story. It made the front page of our *Sunday Republican*. It included a photo of me holding the scrapbook I'd recently made which included photos of my adoptive and biological families. It was taken in my office at school, with all of the photos of my birth family in the background. The second page of the article included a photo of my siblings with me the first time we all were all together.

Barb, Randy, and Shelly. Photo from the *Sunday Republican*

The story read as follows:

Finding Parents, Journey of Faith

Bea O'Quinn Dewberry

Sunday, November 14, 2004

SPRINGFIELD—After 23 years, Barbara Gowan was finally connecting with the voice she had longed to hear since she was a girl.

Would it be cool and distant or warm and loving? Would the connection abruptly end with the sound of a dial tone or be the start of a relationship she yearned for?

Gowan, a 41-year-old married mother of four, knew she was biracial and that the racial climate four decades ago couldn't have been easy for a white mother and black father.

After half a lifetime of searching for the woman who carried her in her womb only to let her go, she told her mother she had had a good life. And then she heard the tears on the other end of the phone.

"I was so nervous and so excited because I had waited my whole life to find her," said Gowan, a nurse at New Leadership Charter School. "My whole body was nervous, excited, anxious as she picked up the phone. My fear was she would say it was not her or say 'I never want to talk to you again.'"

By the grace of God, Gowan said, that didn't happen. And by the grace of God, she said, she found her father. She is writing a book about her journey, but the fairy tale ending that came with finding her parents has a sad footnote. Her mother told her she has lung cancer, but she also told her that knowing what happened to her daughter answered a prayer.

Gowan's successful search for her parents came despite the fact that Massachusetts is one of many states that seals birth records of adopted babies. But that may soon change if a bill to be refiled next month by state Sen. Susan Fargo, D-Lincoln, is approved.

The bill has the support of state Reps. Benjamin Swan, D-Springfield; Gale D. Candaras, D-Wilbraham; and state Sens. Stanley C. Rosenberg, D-Amherst; and Stephen M. Brewer, D-Barre. Similar bills are proposed in New York and New Jersey. In New Hampshire, an open birth records law will take effect Jan. 3. But the National Council for Adoption is opposed to such measures, saying such legislation "unjustly and unnecessarily disrupts the lives of innocent people."

Gowan found her parents despite those obstacles. Her mother is a 60-year-old married mother of two living in Las Vegas, and her father, James E.LeFlore, is a 65-year-old father of two living in New York.

Gowan's relationship with her birth father, LeFlore, a professor at the State University of New York in Oswego, N.Y., has been strong and steady.

When Gowan first contacted LeFlore, he was not aware that he had a child outside the two he had fathered in his first marriage." That initial feeling was a great surprise, shock in fact, as one might imagine to hear that I had a child of (age) 40 that I knew nothing about," LeFlore said.

The two continued telephone conversations, and at the urging of his two children, a blood test was performed.

"I was hoping it would come back positive," LeFlore said. "It's worked out beautifully. She's come here and met my children, and it's all been very exciting." Gowan now calls him "Dad."

Gowan's journey began Oct. of 1963, when her 19-year-old white birth mother was forced to give her up, a black child born out of wedlock. "This will be a book about relinquishment, race and healing," said Gowan. "I want other people in my shoes to have the courage to look, to seek out their relatives, to see that it's possible to finally find some completion," she said. "I want people to see the good side. There's so much stigma attached to adoption. It doesn't need to be a shameful thing."

Gowan's book will also explore the frustrations of searching for a birth parent, including blank leads, closed doors and sealed records. Gowan said she hopes her story will help remove the stigma of adoption and lessen the guilt and shame experienced by birth mothers.

Gowan's desire to search for her mother began early on after her adopted mother, Thelma Miller, told her the name of her birth mother.

At 18, she contacted Child and Family Services to get information. "In my naiveté, I thought maybe she was looking for me too," Gowan said.

Through the years, Gowan contacted child welfare agencies and adoption resource organizations and even hired Adoption USA to find her mother.

"They sent me 500 names and expected me to call them," Gowan said of Adoption USA.

This year in March she struck gold. She contacted an Internet site that guaranteed success in finding a birth parent; if not, the search would be free.

Gowan submitted her request on a Friday morning. By 3:30 that afternoon, they notified her they had found 12 pages of information. The cost would be $1,900.

Gowan sought the advice of her husband, Joey, and prayed to God for an answer, which she said came the following Sunday in church. She paid the fee.

The report revealed her mother lived in Las Vegas. Gowan called her March of 2004, on her son John's birthday.

After the initial shock, her birth mother shared that she was a student attending Syracuse University when she got pregnant by LeFlore. Her parents found out and moved her to an uncle's home in Agawam to have the baby.

Gowan's birth mother went to the hospital alone. "That broke my heart," Gowan said.

Gowan's birth mother had named her Tanya Elizabeth and asked that she be raised by black parents. She held Gowan for a few minutes before a nurse took her away.

Two days after birth, Gowan was released to a foster family. At 10 months, she was adopted by Thelma and Harold Miller, a young black couple living in Springfield. The Millers are both deceased.

Gowan remembers every detail about her first conversation with her birth mother, who wants to remain anonymous.

"I had a list of questions I wanted to ask her. The first one was 'Does anyone know about me?' She said, 'My husband and my daughter, but they don't know you're black.'"

Gowan has struggled all her life with being a biracial child. She often denied her "white side" when people questioned her heritage.

Like most adoptees, Gowan wanted to know the root of her personal and physical characteristics: Who has the cleft chin? The pointy nose? The dark hair? The "brains" that led her to be an honors student and class valedictorian in high school?

Gowan said her birth mother told her she had been diagnosed with lung cancer last year and was saddened to think she might die without having known what happened to her first child.

"I melted," Gowan said. "She said she always wanted to know what happened to me, but she didn't think she had the right to look for me."

Gowan said she told her birth mother she had had a good life and wanted for nothing, even now. "She started crying," Gowan said.

That initial telephone conversation grew into more conversations and eventually the exchange of photographs, including one taken of Gowan's birth mother while a student at Syracuse University. She was four months pregnant at the time. Gowan finally found someone she resembled; her mother has the cleft chin, chubby cheeks and round eyes that sparkle. Her father has the pointy nose.

Essential medical history was shared, as well. Like her mother, Gowan developed arthritis at a young age. Like her father, she has colitis.

Gowan communicates with her maternal sister by e-mail often. Conversations with her birth mother have dwindled some. Gowan speaks to her birth mother at least once a month now.

That's OK, Gowan said. "I kind of try to see how she's feeling. I don't want to put her off, make her feel bad, or feel guilty. I wanted to find her, to see if she looks like me. I kind of satisfied that desire," Gowan said.

"She says she wants to meet me someday. I figure she's not ready now," Gowan said. "Still, even for her, it's been a healing."

Susan C. Dark, the director and founder of the Adoption Connection, a non-profit search organization in Peabody, said adoptees must understand why they were relinquished by a parent in the first place.

"When all this was happening, it wasn't 2004 and morals and society were really different then," said Dark, 60, who is both an adoptee and a birth parent who gave up her son at age 17.

Dark found her birth parents in 1972 and her son in 1980. She said more and more men these days are searching for birth parents.

Gowan has developed a close relationship with her father's son, Randy, and a growing friendship with his daughter, Michelle. Her closest relative has been an aunt Loretta in Baltimore.

Gowan, her husband and four children spent Father's Day with LeFlore at a family gathering. LeFlore came to Springfield on Mother's Day bearing roses and a gift.

LeFlore says he feels no anger toward Gowan's birth mother for not revealing she had borne him a child. He understands why, at that time, a period of racial unrest and sexism, she would have made the choice she did.

As for Gowan, LeFlore says he loves her like any father would. He is proud of her accomplishments and is concerned for her and her family's well-being.

Life for Gowan has been good. Especially in October, she said. "Because it was my first birthday since finding everyone, it was so emotional. My father wrote in a card that this is the first birthday he could say, 'Happy birthday, dearest daughter,'" Gowan said.

Her birth mother mailed a card and an assortment of hand-made crocheted items including a pot holder, sun-catchers and an angel. "I went from not having anyone and being an only child in a small family to having all these people embracing me," Gowan said.

"I really believe the Lord has blessed me because I'm walking in God's will."

After that story ran, I received a very strange visit. Shortly before Christmas, I came home to hear my daughters tell me about an old white man who came by the house and range the bell saying, "Is your mother at home?"

"No," they answered. He then paused.

"I have something for her," he replied.

"You can leave whatever it is with us," they answered. He hesitated again and began looking at the map in his hand.

"No, never mind," he said quickly and left without saying who he was or if he would return. He waited outside of the house for a brief period of time, then left. When I returned home, Brittany recounted the story to me and said she was afraid. The man seemed a bit strange. She even thought about calling the police. After all of the terror alerts, she worried about what was in the envelope or package he had for me. She actually got me nervous thinking about it. About an hour later, he returned. He knocked on the door but I looked through the side window and asked what he wanted. He did look a bit strange and seemed very vague.

"Are you Barbara Gowan?" he asked.

"Yes, who are you?" I answered.

"It doesn't matter who I am. I was told to give this to you," he replied.

"Who sent you to deliver something to me?" I said.

He remained silent.

"I have something to give to you," he said once again. The whole visit had me feeling uneasy. I often open the door to strangers and our neighborhood is very safe and friendly. I probably wouldn't have been suspicious at all had Brittany not been so afraid after his visit. I never opened the door since he wouldn't tell me who sent him or what the "something" was. I actually felt strange being so distant with him and hoped he didn't think I was rude, but I was erring on the side of caution this time. I told him that if he had something to give me, he could leave it on my front steps and I would retrieve it after he left. He looked at me with no emotion and left the white envelope on my front steps and simply said, "I would open it right away if I were you," and left. He was an old white man driving an old car and that is all that I can remember about him.

I opened the door after he drove away and picked up the envelope. It had a map printed from the Mapquest web site in it, with my address and directions to my home. Enclosed in the map were ten one-hundred-dollar bills. To this day, I don't know who sent me the money or who the man was. I asked members of my church and my father's family. They all denied sending me the money. I even wondered if someone from my birth mother's family might have sent it since they had some part in the process of my adoption and she did have a relative who lived in Massachusetts. I later realized that she probably didn't tell them that I had found her. I decided to stop trying to figure it out. Someone wanted me to be blessed during that holiday season. Maybe it was because we were tithing. I will never know where that blessing came from. I decided to just be grateful for it. I was also blessed with many phone calls after that newspaper article ran.

People called to share their stories with me and some simply wanted to talk to someone like them. Some were looking for help in their searches, and some felt they needed to call just to let me know they were moved to tears when reading my story. It was those calls that led me to get busy writing this book. If a news article could elicit that kind of response, then what possibilities were there in a book? I set out to make contacts with others who had walked in my shoes to get their points of view.

I began with a biracial girl in my school whose white parents adopted many mixed-race children. This family struck me as special from the first time I met them. Yolanda was very light-skinned and if not for her thick hair, she probably could have been mistaken for white. Her father is a physician who could probably afford to send her to private school, but she attends my school, which has over 90% students of color. She doesn't have to worry about seeing people who look like her. She has friends of all different races and is encouraged to be herself. All of the children are raised to be proud of who they are. Yolanda's self-confidence amazes me when I compare her with myself at that age. I thought that being raised in a black family would have given me her kind of positive self-image, but it didn't.

I later found out that her adoptive mother was sensitive to adoption issues because she had given up a child for adoption when she was young. She found the child she gave up for adoption, but was rejected by that child. She knows how painful rejection can be and doesn't want her children to ever experience it. She expects that they will have a natural curiosity about their biological backgrounds. She is supportive of whatever decisions they make. She also realizes that their needs don't overshadow their love and appreciation for her. What a gift for an adoptive parent to give a child.

Some of my friends have become adoptive parents. Veronica adopted a beautiful little girl who was a patient of ours in the hospital for almost a year. Her biological mother tried to take care of her but couldn't. She went into foster care. Her foster mother also wanted to adopt her but couldn't. Veronica's entire family has helped and supported her as she became a single parent in adopting Patrice. She didn't do it because she couldn't have children. She now has a biological son. With Veronica's help, Patrice has grown into a healthy, happy, beautiful young girl who has the love of God in her heart.

Another close friend, Dana, has two biological sons. She and her husband chose to give a loving home to a child in need instead of having another biological child. They felt that God wanted them to share their abundant blessings. The child they adopted had a troubled past and was in a foster home with a family that loved her but was unable to adopt her. She is another example of love overcoming the trauma of her past. She does well in school, is happy and healthy, and also has the love of the Lord planted in her heart.

The Alston Family: Dave, Dana, Jordan, Alexandria and Tyler

An old colleague, a white nurse, fell in love with two HIV-positive mixed-race girls who needed a home. She adopted them and was able to love and care for them until they died. What a difference she made in their lives. Another former colleague, also a white woman, had a child of her own but also adopted two black children. She often asked me questions about how best to support their positive self-image. She and the other nurse surrounded these adopted children with friends of all races in order to help them see that love is colorblind. I share these stories about the people in my small circle of friends and coworkers in the hope that they will help dispel many of the myths surrounding adoptive families. Adoptive families are formed for as many reasons as biological families, not only because of infertility, or as a last resort for having children.

In order to gain a male perspective on race and adoption, I interviewed a biracial man who describes himself as "being mistaken for Hispanic or black." He says he has been viewed as having the arrogance of a white man with the anger of a black man. A white family that thought they were infertile adopted him as a young child. They later had four biological children. His adoptive father is a minister. He says they never discussed race. He was expected to be like his siblings. But he wasn't. He was not white. He had problems with his identity and didn't know where he fit in. Most of his elementary school friends were white. He made more black friends in middle school, and even more in high school. This mirrored my experience.

He was unable to confront and understand his issues of rejection and racial identity until he became an adult. He learned that his grandfather and great-grandfather didn't approve of his adoption. They referred to him as a nigger behind his back. He recalls getting beatings as a child while his siblings did not. On one occasion, he was told that he was a bad influence on his siblings when they began to be interested in black music or dating other black teens. When he began dating a white girl, his father wasn't pleased and asked him, "What do you see in white women?" His response to his father was, "What do *you* see in white women?" He was shocked to realize his father didn't approve of him dating a white girl despite the fact that both his biological mother and his adoptive mother were white, and he had been raised in an upper-middle-class, white environment. It was one of his first slaps in the face.

He was kicked out of his home at age fifteen. His best friend's family, who were black, took him in. He says he didn't completely associate himself with the black race until he entered the military. He thought like many biracial people that the rest of the world sees them as black only. Unfortunately, he experienced some rejection from blacks in the military because he spent time with white officers who shared his love of art and chess. He has a child with a biracial woman but says he will date women of any race.

He has had to deal with white friends and colleagues who seemingly accept him but will call other blacks niggers. When confronted about this, they say, "But you're not like them, you are different!" This reminded me of some of the things that were said to me.

He had no contact with his adoptive family for 10 years. He calls his adoptive father by his first name, which they feel is disrespectful. He says "I will call him dad when he starts acting like my dad." He admits that his friend's father is more of a father figure to him than is his adoptive dad. He continues to have conflicting opinions on their current relationship and where it should go. He also has conflicting feelings about whether to search for his birth family. He and I share the belief that self-analysis is critical to growth. We also agree that we need to be open and honest with ourselves before we can be open and honest with others.

I gained a unique perspective from a transracially adopted, biracial thirty-nine-year-old woman who is married to a black physician. They are in the process of adopting a child of their own. She lived in a large family that consisted of adopted and biological children. The adopted children were multiracial. She said that her parents went out of their way to expose them to black culture. Her friendships changed as she was exposed to different cultures as she moved from elementary through high school. Her experiences mirrored those of other adoptees already mentioned. She agrees that as a biracial population, we experience similar things.

We discussed the need for problems to be examined in the context of co-existing problems such as developmental level and environment. For example, when my mother was angry with me and said, "If you act up, I will send you back to Brightside!" I took it as rejection because I was adopted. This adopted woman pointed out that my mother might also have said something like that to a biological child. Also, most teenagers have questions about their identity and fitting in. These are a natural part of growing up. Our particular problems and questions may have focused on race and adoption, but other teens may focus on other aspects of identity. This adoptee says she was curious about her birth mother but didn't feel like something was missing in her life if she never met her. Her birth mother, siblings, and grandparents were found, however, as a result of a search that was encouraged and supported by her adoptive parents. She sees her birth family as distant relatives. She cares about them, but feels more of a connection to her adoptive family. We share the view that there is a need for education with regard to issues of race and adoption.

She has been involved in educating prospective adoptive parents about the needs of adopted children, especially those who are considering transracial adoption. She believes that many families do not understand the role that race plays in our society as a whole and that although love is clearly the most important element of family, simply loving a child and ignoring the child's race may cause some serious problems. She summarized by saying that she works with families to encourage awareness about the need to expose children to a diversity of experiences and people so they can develop individual interests and a healthy self-identity.

To get a perspective on adoption and race from someone who wasn't adopted but was involved with adoption, I contacted a Chicago adoption attorney named Michelle Hughes, a biracial woman who runs Bridge Communications. She has been instrumental in educational as well as social gatherings for those touched by adoption and those in the multicultural and biracial communities. She began doing this when she saw the need in this sort of community. Her gatherings are the perfect outlet for others to share their experiences and for education about transracial adoptions.

Ms. Hughes notes that her friends belong to all cultures. She has also had to deal with the constant questions about her ethnicity. When asked, she simply says she is black—for the same reasons I did. She says that describing herself as biracial seems to lend credence to some people's notion that her intelligence or attractiveness are supplied by her white genes. I was happily surprised to see I wasn't the only one who'd had that feeling. Stereotyping appears to be just as prevalent now as in our past, despite the growth in the multicultural community.

We discussed the assimilation into the black culture that many white mothers of biracial children go through in order for their children to fit into the black community. She agrees that this is what occurs in most of the interracial marriages that involve the whites and blacks. She notes that this is often due to the fact that the white community has historically had a harder time accepting biracial children than the black community. She has noticed these trends as an adoption attorney.

Ms. Hughes told me she has found that biracial children are proportionately put up for adoption more than black children. White women place biracial children up for adoption more because of their race as well as for the many other reasons that children are placed for adoption. That doesn't seem to be the case with other mixed-race children. Michelle's perspective, as well as that of all of the other people I interviewed, gave me a clearer picture of how adoption affects many members in the adoption triad.

Knowledge is power and education is the key. There are many different opinions about adoption. They often depend upon the person's position in the triad. In the December 12, 2004, issue of *Parade* magazine, I found a small yet important article that finally gave credence to what adoptees have been saying for years. Medical information is important.

The article said that knowing your family tree could save your life: "Some of the biggest health advances are in genetics—and finding the best ways to help patients may lie in knowing their family health histories." It mentioned that diseases such as stroke and diabetes could be genetic. Having family members with diseases such as these can heighten a person's risk of developing them. The Surgeon General recommended that all Americans compile a family health history. The article included a computer program to help. It is called My Family Portrait and can be found at www.hhs.gov/familyhistory.

This is one of the areas where adoptees are often kept in the dark. The health information given at adoption often becomes inaccurate as biological parents age. I was told that there were no hereditary illnesses in my birth family, probably because at age 19 my birth mother didn't know of any. I later learned that there were many such illnesses on both sides of my family tree. Now that I know about them, I am much better equipped to manage my health.

The question I get most often from those who have heard about my discoveries is "When are you going to meet your birth mother?" I used to think that was the sole purpose for my search. I felt like I had to touch her and hug her and speak to her in person. I thought I needed that in order for it to be real for me. It was difficult for me to hear "we will meet someday" and not know if someday would ever come. I'd been hoping for "I can't wait to see you," which is what I got from my birth father. It was as if my birth family had control over my very existence and my destiny.

I realize now that God allowed me to find them. In the past, my self-worth would have been determined by whether my birth family showed me love or if they felt I was worthy of acknowledgment. I know now that I am a child of God and I was not a mistake. I am here for a purpose and my value isn't tied to anyone else's approval of me. What a long journey I had to take to discover these things.

Christmas 2006

Epilogue

"All of that for this" ...

December 31, 2006, New Year's Eve sermon, St. John's Congregational Church, Springfield, Massachusetts: The choir sang, the gospel comedian made us laugh, and our pastor delivered a powerful message. He said at the onset that the message wasn't for everyone, but I knew he was speaking to me. Among other things, he talked about the struggles many of us went through in 2006 and told us that God can take your pain, your mistakes, your sickness, your faults, and your failures and work them together to allow His glory to shine in your life.

The last two years brought many changes in my life with accompanying joys and pains. India graduated from high school and was accepted to a good college. Sadly, she hasn't been able to fulfill her dream of succeeding in college, as she has been dealing with many personal problems that have become a constant source of depression. Brittany has been struggling with her identity as she enters her senior year of high school and looks forward to graduation and attending a college in the South. JJ and John continue to be happy and healthy while enjoying the carefree lives of children.

I was able to return to the Caribbean twice and spend quality time with my friends and children over the past two years. While there I did a lot of soul searching, and reached a turning point after returning from my last trip to Jamaica. Veronica and I were finishing up last-minute preparations for her wedding. I was excited about her upcoming nuptials and looked forward to serving as her maid of honor and giving the toast at her wedding. We reminisced about how I'd introduced her to her fiancé three years earlier and how their relationship progressed. With this joyful event came the realization that my own marriage wasn't what a healthy Christian marriage should be. I had to face the fact that even when two people love each other, they may not be able to make a marriage work if they don't have the same priorities. I knew in my heart that we had to go our separate ways before resentment and anger destroyed what we managed to keep together for eleven years.

We parted as friends. Joey was finally able to lead a more carefree life on the road, driving trucks without a wife monitoring his smoking and spending habits. We could also stop arguing about how his unfair and sometimes abusive treatment of my girls was affecting our family. He could now control his own destiny. He no longer had to make excuses for why he couldn't make time for his family. He now had a valid excuse—he was working and on the road. I was often told that God doesn't have to fix what He didn't put together.

I received a popular email recently from a friend that spoke about how some people come into your life for a reason, some for a season, and some for a lifetime. It is not always up to us how long each person is in our life as it takes two people to maintain a relationship.

The relationship with my birth mother is one that has brought me great joy and great pain. I believe Joanne was meant to be in my life for a reason and a season. I am grateful that she gave me life, and for a brief season she was able to give me the answers and comfort I needed. However, her calls stopped over a year ago. I have come to terms with the reality that I may never meet her. My birth father reminds me that I need to let her reach out if she wants a relationship with me. I continue to send cards on her birthday, Mother's Day, and Christmas, but the last card I received from her or her daughter was over a year ago on Christmas.

I no longer pray for God to intervene in our meeting, but only for her to be happy and healthy. I spent a lot of time lamenting over her reluctance to meet me or continue our relationship; but I now trust that whether we ever meet or not will be the Will of God and whatever He has in store for me will be much greater than what I planned for myself.

In spite of how things have turned out, I am still sure that I made the right decision to find her and it gave me the closure I needed in that area of my life. It also led me to my birth father.

The relationship with my birth father's family continues to evolve. I have maintained contact with all of my new family members and have grown especially close to my brother over this last year. Many of the issues I struggle with that I used to attribute to my adoption are those I share with him. My father told me that Randy and I were very much alike even before I met him. We have been able to support each other a great deal this year and are trying to make family time more of a priority in all of our lives.

I was feeling like a failure at the end of 2006 as I looked back over the last year of my life. Having two marriages fail isn't anything anyone would choose. I realize now that both husbands had a season and God didn't choose either one of them. I did the choosing both times, and jumped in quickly while ignoring all of the warning signs. The only thing that mattered to me was "Do you love me?" It takes more than love to sustain any relationship. If I had realized this in my 20s and 30s, I probably wouldn't have married either husband as quickly as I did. I married Pete within six months of reuniting with him, and married Joey less than five months after getting back together with him. I should have waited to get to know each of them better while working on many of the basic issues that most pastors discuss in premarital counseling. Maybe that would have made a difference, maybe not. I also realize that I wasted many years trying to help them with their problems when I may have been doing more harm than good by enabling their destructive or counterproductive behavior. I think of the song *Again*, by Faith Evans: *If I had to do it all again, I wouldn't take away the rain cause I know it made me who I am.* I feel the same way. I am who I am because of my successes as well as my failures. I also have my four precious children who were born as a result of my marriages. I am thankful that I am no longer driven by the need to have a picture-perfect nuclear family in order feel complete.

It is hard to let go of our dreams for ourselves and for our children. In hindsight, I have learned that my desire to make my children always feel loved sometimes interfered with my ability to use consistency in parenting. With my girls, I vacillated from being an overprotective mother, to a strict disciplinarian, to a comforter and counselor. I also gave in too much in an attempt to overcompensate for the love that they didn't receive from their father and grandparents. I pray that none of my children will feel unloved or unwanted by Joey's family due to the breakup of our marriage. Sometimes it is hard for even good people to realize what is best for children when they are dealing with their own emotions. Parenting is a delicate balance. It can be especially difficult without the guidance and support of an extended family. It is true what they say about it taking a village to raise a child. Parenting has become easier for me as I learned to accept the love and support of those who make up my village.

I felt that because I was so blessed with friends and family, I needed to reach out to others and be a blessing to them. I found myself giving a home to two teenage girls who had no place to live at a time that I should have been focusing on my own teenage daughters. The two girls had a season in my home. They have both moved on and I learned lessons from that experience. My last lesson came at the year's end when I allowed a person camouflaged as a friend into my life. It was hard for me to admit to myself that some people are not who they appear to be and that some may even befriend you for their own selfish reasons, and may not have your best interests at heart. I have tried to live by the principle, "Do unto others as you want them to do unto you." I will continue to live by that principle but will be more careful when choosing those I allow into my life. Veronica repeatedly tells me, "You can't keep doing things the same way and expect different results."

As I listened to two sermons in church on New Year's Eve and a broadcast from Joel Osteen on television that night, I heard one constant theme. Sometimes God will allow you to keep making the same mistakes over and over again until you suffer enough to do things His way, and not your way. It takes longer for some of us to find the lesson in the journey than others. I was able to find solace with the beginning of the New Year. I have come to realize that we all have issues. Mine may not be yours, and yours may not be mine. Many of us look outside of ourselves to find happiness. I used to think, "I'll be happy when I go away to college, get married, have a child of my own, find my birth mother," and on and on and on. Many of these things did bring me happiness, but what is more important is the inner peace and joy I found when I learned to be content in whatever situation I am in.

It is important to strive for peace even if things don't go your way. I have peace in knowing that sometimes to love someone is to accept them as they are, even if it means letting them make their own mistakes and lead their own lives. I also have peace with the realization that I am a whole, complete person, and my family and the circumstances of my birth don't define my value. More important, I have grown to see that family relationships aren't based on marriage or birth but by shared experiences and the love felt by those around you.

Finally, I have learned that surviving trials, and finding the lessons in them, can be a testimony to others. We need to let go of the guilt and condemnation we often feel in our failures and learn to forgive others as well as forgiving ourselves. My trials have led me to understand myself as well as my purpose in life, an important part of which is sharing my journey in the hope that it will inspire those seeking a relationship with God to find a church home. I now have an inner peace despite not knowing what my future holds. I realize I am a work in progress and am striving to just be the best "me" I can be. I work daily on recognizing my blessings, which include the many people who came into my life for a brief season as well as those I hope to have with me for a lifetime.

It is my prayer that other adoptees and multicultural families will find solace in my story. I pray that they can find peace with the circumstances of their birth. I want to scream to everyone, "You were not an accident, regardless of the circumstances of your birth!" I believe that every person was created for a purpose. It is often difficult to figure out what that purpose is; but I do believe that we are not here simply to satisfy our own worldly desires. We are here to affect and be affected by others.

One adoptee helped me see that all of my life, I have been trying to "blend in" with those around me. I now realize that I am who I am because of a blend of my biological parents, adoptive parents, and all of the other people who were and are a part of my life. I can stop searching and trying to fit in. I am OK just as I am. When I think of the words "family" and "home," I think of a place where a person is truly understood and accepted, valued, and unconditionally loved. In that respect, I have found my home and my family.

One evening, as I was working on the final touches for this book, my son JJ, now age ten, was in my room drawing, as he does every night before our nightly prayers. He looked over at me and said "Thank you, Mommy."

I didn't know why he said that, out of the blue, so I said, "Thank you for what JJ?"

He paused; then smiled and simply said, "Everything!"

That touched my heart and reminded me of what unconditional love and appreciation is all about. That is exactly how I feel about the special people in my life and the value of God's presence in my life.

In this journey of mine toward healing, I found it helpful to read adoption books and talk with other adoptees about concerns I previously had been too afraid to discuss openly. I thought my feelings were unique to me until I came in contact with others with stories like my own. The appendix has a list of adoption books and resources that I hope will provide information, support, and guidance to those who need it. I have also included books that have helped me to heal some of my lifelong issues that were rooted in my childhood. These are books that were recommended by my Christian counselor, Minister Gregory Jones.

I pray that biological parents will become more informed about their choices. There are decisions to be made about open and closed adoptions; there is a way to get medical information to a child years after the adoption is final; there are ways to contact adopted children even after the adoption is final. Finally, I pray that all adoptive parents will seek out information and support regarding the special and specific needs of their adoptive children, and themselves, and that they will understand the cultural and emotional needs of their children. Sherrie Eldridge's book, *Twenty Things Adopted Kids Wish Their Adoptive Parents Knew*, is a great start. I found it helpful and gave it to my friends with adopted children.

My secret for finding peace was not in finding my biological parents and their families. My faith in God, His unconditional love, grace, mercy, and His strength has been what has been my greatest source of healing. He made it possible for me to find my birth family, but it happened exactly when and how it was supposed to happen, and not how or when I wanted it.

Kirk Franklin wrote a song entitled *Imagine Me* that I feel epitomizes my life. His song is about learning to love yourself and being set free from insecurities, being strong, and letting go of the hurts of the past. It is also about how trusting God will allow you to no longer live in fear but in His love. The lyrics to this song and his powerful music video have given me great comfort during this time of self-evaluation and healing.

For the first time in my life, I am now excited about traveling through the rest of my life despite not knowing what my future holds. More important, I am willing to trust God, and let him be in the driver's seat.

APPENDIX

Resources for Adoptive Families

Books About Adoption

Boss, Pauline, *Ambiguous Loss: Learning to Live With Unresolved Grief*, Harvard University Press (Oct. 2, 2000)

Brooks, Thomas, *A., Wealth of Family: An Adopted Son's International Quest for Heritage, Reunion, and Enrichment*, Houston, Alpha Multimedia, Inc. (Aug. 1, 2006)

Eldridge, Sherrie, *Twenty Things Adopted Kids Wish Their Adoptive Parents Knew*, New York, Dell Publishing (Oct. 12, 1999)

Eldridge, Sherrie, *Twenty Life Transforming Choices Adoptees Need to Make*, Colorado Springs, Pinon Press (April 2003)

Jones, Merry Bloch, *Birthmothers: Women Who Have Relinquished Babies for Adoption Tell Their Stories*, Backinprint.com (August 2000)

McKinley, Catherine E., *The Book of Sarahs: A Family in Parts*, New York, Counterpoint (Oct. 21, 2003)

Verrier, Nancy Newton, *The Primal Wound: Understanding The Adopted Child*, Baltimore, Gateway Press (April 1993)

Books About Multiculturalism

Lewis, Elliot, *Fade: My Journeys in Multiracial America*, New York, Carroll & Graf (Dec. 8, 2006)

McBride, James, *The Color of Water: A Black Man's Tribute to His White Mother*, New York, Riverhead Books (1996)

Root, Maria, and Kelly, Matt, Ed., *Multicultural Child Resource Book*, Seattle, WA, Mavin Foundation (2003)

Books About Faith

Meyers, Joyce, *In Pursuit of Peace: 21 Ways to Conquer Anxiety, Fear, and Discontentment*, New York, Warner Faith (Sept. 7, 2004)

Omartian, Stormie, *The Power of a Praying Woman*, Eugene, OR, Harvest House Publishers (July 1, 2002)

Omartian, Stormie, *The Power of a Praying Parent*, Eugene, OR, Harvest House Publishers (July 1, 2005)

Peterson, Eugene H., *The Message: The Bible in Contemporary Language*, Navpress Publishing Group (Jan. 22, 2007)

Warren, Rick, *The Purpose Driven Life: What on Earth Am I Here For?* Grand Rapids, MI, Zondervan (2002)

Books About Healing

Beattie, Melody, *Codependent No More: How to Stop Controlling Others and Start Caring for Yourself*, HarperSanFrancisco (1992)

Meyers, Joyce, *Beauty for Ashes: Receiving Emotional Healing*, New York, Faith-Words (Nov. 1, 2003)

Seamands, David A., *Healing for Damaged Emotions*, Colorado Springs, Life Journey (September 1991)

Whitfield, Charles L., M.D., *Boundaries and Relationships*, Deerfield Beach, FL, Health Communications Inc. (April 1, 1994)

Whitfield, Charles L., M.D., *Healing the Child Within: Discovery and Recovery for Adult Children of Dysfunctional Families*, Deerfield Beach, FL, Health Communications Inc. (1987)

Web Sites

www.adoption.com—An independent adoption center with links to many other sites.

www.adoptioncrossroads.org—Search and support network for adoptees and birthparents seeking reunion.

www.adoptionjewels.org—Faith-based, quarterly e-newsletters and a bulletin board.

www.adoptionregistry.com—The largest on-line adoption reunion registry

www.adoptionweek.com—Register here for a weekly e-magazine

www.christianadoptions.com—Faith-based site offering daily devotionals and articles.

www.tapestrybooks.com—On-line catalogue of adoption books.

Organizations

The American Adoption Congress (AAC)
P.O. Box 42730
Washington, DC 20015
202-483-3399
Seminars, networking, support groups, and conventions for adoptees.

Association of MultiEthnic Americans, Inc. (AMEA)
P.O. Box 341304
Los Angeles, CA 90034-1304
www.ameasite.org

Bridge Communications, Inc.
221 N. LaSalle, Suite 2020
Chicago, IL 60601
312-377-2748
www.bridgecommunications.org

Mavin Foundation
600 First Avenue, Suite 600
Seattle, WA 98104-2215
206-622-7101
www.mavinfoundation.org

Pact, An Adoption Alliance
4179 Piedmont Avenue, Suite 330
Oakland, CA 94611
510-243-9460
www.pactadopt.org

978-0-595-44385-7
0-595-44385-0